VEGGIE
BURGER ATELIER

Brimming with creative inspiration, how-to projects, and useful information to enrich your everyday life, Quarto Knows is a favorite destination for those pursuing their interests and passions. Visit our site and dig deeper with our books into your area of interest: Quarto Creates, Quarto Cooks, Quarto Homes, Quarto Lives, Quarto Drives, Quarto Explores, Quarto Gifts, or Quarto Kids.

10 9 8 7 6 5 4 3 2 1

ISBN: 978-1-63159-348-2

Digital edition published in 2018

Library of Congress Cataloging-in-Publication Data

Olsson, Nina, author.
Veggie burger atelier / photography and recipes by Nina Olsson.
ISBN 9781631593482 (pbk.)
LCSH: Meat substitutes. | Hamburgers. | Vegetarian cooking. |
LCGFT: Cookbooks.
LCC TX838 .O47 2017 | DDC 641.5/636--dc23

LCCN 2017030194

Design & Page Layout: Nina Olsson
Photography: Nina Olsson

Printed in China

Please see your health care provider before beginning any new health program.

VEGGIE
BURGER ATELIER

EXTRAORDINARY RECIPES FOR NOURISHING PLANT-BASED
PATTIES, PLUS BUNS, CONDIMENTS, AND SWEETS

NINA OLSSON

Contents

WHY I WROTE A BOOK STARRING VEGGIE BURGERS

In my opinion, veggie burgers really have it all—fun layers of delicious flavors in perfect harmony. When my editor Jonathan at Quarry Books approached me to discuss a possible book, it was soon clear that—YES!—my love for veggie burgers could be turned into a book! Here I've gathered veggie burgers inspired by flavors from around the world. They're all easy to make, deliciously delectable, and made from good-for-you ingredients.

I've been a fan of healthy food for many years and a committed vegetarian with a penchant for turning indulgent fast-food dishes such as pizzas, tacos, and burgers into new and nourishing creations. My family and children are bonkers for veggie burgers and we often whip them up together and enjoy real "happy meals" at home. Many people are still under the impression that healthy vegetarian food is boring, and it's always lovely to see the look on their faces as they chew into a perfectly layered veggie burger—especially that moment of surprise when they realize it's really delicious when made right.

A veggie burger wasn't always the star dish it is now. Its rise is much like the famous children's story "The Ugly Duckling," who grew into a beautiful swan—once belittled but now a shining star. In the years before the new wave of vegetarianism exploded on food blogs and social media platforms, veggie burgers weren't worth much in public opinion. A veggie burger was usually considered just a sad food choice—soggy, tasteless, and uninspiring were adjectives commonly used to describe it.

That's history—the veggie burger has come a long way during the past few years. It is now one of the most-talked-about and hippest things on the table, and every chef with a reputation is churning out unique versions of plant-based burgers for enthusiastic eaters. People are queuing up for veggie burgers as they would for a pop concert, and for good reasons—with so many people interested in eating greener and healthier, the competition for making the most delicious veggie burger has sky rocketed. Veggie burgers are now so delicious and attractive that it's not only vegetarians who eat them but also meat eaters, who may actually prefer a veggie burger to a meat burger in this brave new world.

But hype and trendiness aside, what I love about veggie burgers is how versatile and creative they are—offering endless possibilities and variations to enjoy. Mastering veggie burgers is about understanding the alchemy of plants. This book shows you how to easily create veggie burgers with a variety of flavor combinations.

HOW TO USE THIS BOOK

The recipes in this book are designed to be easy to follow and adaptable. If you're missing a particular spice or grain, don't let it stop you from cooking the recipes—substitute what you have that's similar. Many recipes are suitable for vegans or can be easily adjusted to be.

You'll also find a variety of sauces, dips, and toppings that can be combined freely. The burgers are inspired by different kitchens from around the world, but mixing and matching as you like is a great way to enjoy these culinary creations!

FORK OR FOOD PROCESSOR

Making the mix: The majority of patties in the book are made with a mixture of ingredients. There is more than one way to make the patties, and feel free to choose whatever method fits you best. You can easily make the mixtures by using your hands, a fork, or a food processor. If you are using your hands or a fork to combine the mixture, cut pieces of fried mushrooms and chunky vegetables smaller before mixing in a bowl, and use a fork to mash and break up beans before mixing with other ingredients. If you use a food processor, be careful so as not to over blend the mixtures.

SHAPING PATTIES

When shaping the patties, using your hands is easy. You can also use metal rings and stuff these with patty mixture. Use a spatula to transfer the patties to a frying pan and later on to the burger breads.

OVEN OR PAN

All panfried patties can also be baked in the oven. I usually prefer the frying pan because it gives a firmer and crustier texture, but the oven is a great option if you are insecure about handling the patties in the pan. Frying patties is an acquired skill; once you make a few you'll have it in your system and, just like making perfect pancakes, practice makes perfect. For the best results, fry one patty at

the time. Patties are always the best served warm straight after cooking.

TIMES AND TEMPERATURES

You don't need to let the patty mixture rest in the fridge before shaping and frying, but it makes the mixture easier and firmer to work with. Times in the frying pan can vary across different stoves, and the given temperature will have different results in different homes. Watch your patties as they brown to avoid burning them. Because the patties are not meat based they don't have to be cooked through in the same way as meat burgers. They only need to be hot and have an appetizing surface, so there's no exact science to worry about. Trust your own senses when frying delicious veggie burgers!

GLUTEN-FREE BURGERS

The toppings and suggestions in the book are all interchangable for your own favorites. Use gluten-free bread or other alternatives to bread such as avocado, rice, or portobello mushrooms as your buns. When soy sauce is listed in the ingredients list, use tamari sauce or gluten-free soy sauce instead. All patties made from a mixture can easily be rolled into vegetarian meatballs, or use them in salads or gluten-free grain bowls.

VEGAN

Wherever dairy or cheese is listed in the ingredients list, you can substitute it with a vegan alternative.

VEGGIE BURGER BASICS

THE ANATOMY OF A PERFECT VEGGIE BURGER

The recipes in this book are all fairly flexible. You can easily exchange ingredients for similar ones and choose to use a fork and your hands instead of a food processor when making the patties. Learn how to adjust the mixtures for best hold, taste, and juiciness in this chapter. At the end of the book, you'll find a handy cheat sheet with guidance on different ingredients and how they work in your veggie burgers.

Anyone can master the art of making outstanding veggie burgers. This chapter guides you through the use of ingredients and techniques.

Let's start the burger flipping!

basics

—

THE FOUR ELEMENTS

The key to making great-tasting veggie burgers is understanding the four basic elements that build the perfect veggie burger: texture, flavor, firmness, and juiciness.

I. TEXTURE

A food's texture directly affects its taste. Texture alone has the power to make or break an otherwise well-composed veggie burger. The general rule is that a rougher texture tastes better than a smooth, puréed bite. There are exceptions, of course, such as falafel burgers, where a smooth inside is balanced by a crustier outer surface. When it comes to the crucial part of pulsing the patty mixture in a food processor, remember the motto "less is more." Pulse in batches for only a couple seconds to break up bigger pieces into a crumbly texture.

Using a variety of ingredients makes a compelling texture. Chunky, broken bits of beans and lentils, crushed nuts, stringy onion, and carrots are great, but the real texture stars are bouncy whole grains such as barley, rice, or freekeh. Toasting your grains gives them an extra tasty, nutty bite. For extra crunch, coat your patties with panko bread crumbs or toasted bread crumbs.

The bun itself also plays a huge part in the tasting experience of the whole burger. A bun with a thin, hard crust and rather light whole grain, soft inside has an ideal texture that complements many types of patties.

2. FLAVOR

Plant-based patties are mostly blank canvases when it comes to flavor, so spices and other flavor boosters are needed. The most important flavor for savory satisfaction is umami, one of the five basic human tastes. While meat and seafood are packed with umami, plant-based patties need a bit more, so be creative. Soy, mushrooms, sun-dried tomatoes, garlic, onions, nuts, toasted sesame oil, and nutritional yeast are plant-based umami ingredients popular in vegan cooking. Vegetarians can also boost umami flavor by adding dairy cheeses and using ghee for frying.

Using ingredients with distinct flavors, such as cauliflower and fennel, adds interest to veggie burgers. Herbs and spices also add plenty of interest and character, so use them generously.

Human taste buds are designed to love food that's been heated, touched by fire, or smoked (it helped our ancestors digest foods easier). Liquid smoke (available bottled from natural health stores and specialized culinary stores) adds that extra-smoky taste, or using charred vegetables as part of your toppings or in your patty mixture also adds lots of delicious flavor.

While a flavorful patty is important, it's only one part of the whole burger's taste. Tangy and fresh toppings and sauces balances the patty's flavor. A delicious burger is composed of a harmony of flavors, so mix freshness, spicy, savory, and sourness for the perfect bite.

3. FIRMNESS

When you have the texture and flavor mastered, you'll want to keep the goodness firmly together. Consider the patty mixture's moistness. Veggie burgers are all bout alliances—too

---

PLANT MAGIC!

Combining plant-based ingredients into delicious patties is all about balance. You can easily experiment with making your own patties by combining the four main elements. Check out the Veggie Burger Cheat Sheet on page 154 for an overview.

much moisture makes soggy, heavy burgers that fall apart when handled. If the mixture is too dry, you'll end up with patties that crumble. Fry or roast vegetables, such as mushrooms and eggplant, before adding them to a mixture to reduce their natural moisture. Use sun-dried tomatoes in mixtures or a concentrated paste and save the fresh tomatoes for toppings.

Eggs are frequently used as binder in veggie burgers, but I'm not very fond of adding eggs. I sometimes use *chia eggs*, which are both nourishing and a good binder. To make one chia egg: Soak 1 tablespoon (11 g) chia seeds in 3 tablespoons (45 ml) water and let sit for 15 minutes. It makes a sticky gel substance that blends well with mixtures.

In general, to make patties that hold together well:

1. **Do not overblend the mixture.** A varied texture gives a good hold.
2. **Blend a small portion** of the mixture finer than the rest to help with the rougher portions.
3. **Absorb excess moisture** in a too-wet mixture by adding oats or broken-up grains and always adjust the flavorings when you add bulking ingredients like these.

A veggie burger doesn't need to duplicate the taste and texture of a classic beef burger—rather, it can go in many directions. Sinking your teeth into a soft but textured mushroom burger is heavenly, and there are many looks and consistencies that are equally delicious. One of the most popular ingredients for creating a good hold is black beans. A firm black bean and oat burger could be labeled as a "well-done" burger while a beet and quinoa burger is more closely classified as a "medium-rare" burger, with a softer bite. The easiest way to make a veggie burger that does not fall apart is to make it using a single ingredient. A slice of roasted sweet potato, Halloumi, or beet can easily serve as a delicious, juicy burger between buns and with fresh toppings.

4. JUICINESS

Getting that moisture balance right makes all the difference. Minimize excessive moisture left after cooking, washing, and draining in favor of natural plant juices and other ingredients that add more flavor. Let cooked rice and drained beans dry naturally for 30 minutes, if you have the time—spread them out on a clean kitchen towel or a tray covered with paper towels. Quickly fry just-rinsed ingredients in a dry pan or let them dry for a short while in the oven. Add tastier juiciness to your patty mixture with soy, chili sauces, olive oil, BBQ sauce, or fresh lemon juice. You can also use juicy plants such as beets, zucchini, and carrots. Mushrooms and onions are outstanding for delivering juiciness packed with umami flavor.

In the overall burger experience a great part of the juiciness comes from the sauces and toppings. Simple mayonnaise and Sriracha or ketchup with fresh lettuce and tomatoes or avocado are safe combinations that never fail. Why stop there, though, if burgers are one of your favorite foods? There are plenty of delicious sauces and toppings to keep you interested for a long time.

TOOLS

Use your hands or metal rings to shape patties.

The simplest way to make a veggie burger is using a fork and your hands to combine a mixture of ingredients.

Other useful tools are:

1. Sharp knife
2. Bowl
3. Grater
4. Frying pan with low brim
5. Spatula
6. Scale
7. Measuring cups and spoons
8. Food processor

The Basic Veggie Burger

Making a veggie burger, as you've learned, is easy if you combine the right balance of elements. The following structure is a starting point, or you can create your own combinations based on your taste preferences:

- **Pulses:** Beans or lentils or a mixture of both are a great way to start a veggie burger. Black beans are a reliable choice, but all beans are usually good binders. Use firmer types of lentils. Avoid the soft red lentils; they're usually too mushy.

- **Grains:** Starchy cooked grains such as rice, bulgur, or freekeh are perfect for bite and bulk. Oats and bread crumbs are also perfect fillers. Mixing grains gives a varied texture. Rice and oats are a superb combination.

- **Vegetables:** Sautéed onions, mushrooms, or eggplant add both juiciness and umami-rich savor. Vegetables such as fennel and cauliflower are also a great addition for good taste.

- **Flavor makers:** Garlic, herbs, spices, chiles, soy sauce or tamari, cheeses, nutritional yeast, and other components add delicious flavor. Make sure your burger has a good deal of umami flavor.

BASIC VEGGIE BURGER

PULSES | GRAINS | VEGETABLES | FLAVOR MAKERS

This basic recipe, a mix of pulses, grains, vegetables, and flavor makers, follows the simple structure just outlined. Adjust the amounts of each ingredient group to create a sticky mixture that holds together well. Add more starchy ingredients, such as grains and beans, for a firmer hold, and adjust the amount of flavor makers after tasting. Select your combination of ingredients from the suggestions, or use a variety of similar ingredients to create your own burger.

1. In a large bowl, combine all the patty ingredients, *except* the oil or ghee. Working in batches, pulse the mixture in a food processor for a few seconds to get a crumbly texture—don't over blend into a flour. Transfer each batch back to the bowl. Make a test patty to see how it holds together. Adjust firmness by adding more dry grains if the mixture is too wet; add juicy elements if the mixture is too dry. Taste and adjust the seasonings with salt or other flavoring ingredients if the mixture tastes too plain—make it exciting for your palate.

2. Refrigerate the mixture for 15 minutes, or up to 24 hours covered. Divide the mixture into 4 equal portions and shape each of them into a patty.

3. Place a skillet over medium-high heat and add a drizzle of oil. Fry the patties for 3 to 4 minutes per side until golden. Alternatively, preheat the oven to 375°F (190°C). Place the patties on a rimmed baking sheet and bake for 15 to 20 minutes, carefully flipping halfway through the cooking time.

   You could also use a combination of cooking methods: Preheat the oven to 375°F (190°C) and place a skillet over medium-high heat. Add a drizzle of oil to the skillet and fry the patties carefully 2 to 3 minutes total, turning, until golden. Transfer the patties to a rimmed baking sheet and bake for about 10 minutes, carefully flipping halfway through the cooking time. This method adds a nice frying surface to the burgers and bakes them through.

4. Lightly toast the buns and assemble the burgers with the buns and toppings.

Makes 4 burgers

For Patties

10½ ounces (300 g) roughly chopped sautéed mushrooms, eggplant, onions, or beets, plus more as needed

1⅓ cups (298 g) drained and rinsed canned beans or lentils, mashed with a fork, plus more as needed

About ⅓ cup (2½ ounces, or 70 g) cooked brown rice, bulgur, or freekeh, plus more as needed

About ¼ cup (40 g) rolled oats or other flakes, plus more as needed

3 cloves garlic, crushed

2 tablespoons (8 g) nutritional yeast or grated Parmesan cheese

2 tablespoons (30 ml) soy sauce or tamari

¾ teaspoon salt, plus more to taste

¼ teaspoon freshly ground black pepper, plus more to taste

Herbs, spices, cheeses, or other defining tastes (optional)

Olive oil or ghee, for frying

4 buns, halved and lightly toasted

The Basic Veggie Burger (page 21) with fresh dill, lemon juice, and Mustard Mayo (page 38).

NORTHERN EUROPE

In the north of Europe, the winters are long and cold. Only the toughest vegetables, such as roots, onions, and cabbages, thrive. Despite the harsh climate, northern cooking is far from limited or boring! By making good use of ingredients such as alliums and generous use of chives and dill (a.k.a. "the garlic of the North") there's plenty to enjoy!

Common Nordic grains are spelt, oats, barley, and rye. Mix them with roots, herbs, mushrooms, onions, and nuts, or create a seafood flavor by adding seaweed to your veggie burgers for a distinct Nordic flare.

Nordic dishes often rely on highlights of sourness from ingredients such as pickles, gherkins, and kraut or sweet-and-sour onions. Mustard and horseradish are popular for adding heat!

STROGANOFF BURGER

PIMENTÓN (SMOKED PAPRIKA) | MUSHROOMS | BROWN RICE | GHERKINS

This burger is inspired by the famous Russian dish, stroganoff. Full of warm, smoky paprika flavor, it's not for nothing that this peppery stew is loved far outside the Russian borders. Combining savory mushrooms and tangy lemon juice yields a robust yet tantalizing flavor. Serve with sour cream or yogurt and pickles for a delicious stroganoff experience. This burger is a feast for your taste buds!

1. To make the patties: Preheat the oven to 350°F (180°C). Spread the mushrooms, black beans, and onion on a rimmed baking sheet. Salt lightly and sprinkle with thyme. Roast for 35 minutes, flipping everything after 15 to 20 minutes. Remove the sheet from the oven and let cool. Reduce the temperature to 140°F (60°C).

2. In a food processor, combine the cooled toasted vegetables and roasted red bell pepper. Pulse a few times into smaller pieces. Transfer to a large bowl and add the remaining patty ingredients (through salt). Taste and adjust the seasoning with pepper and more salt if needed. Refrigerate for 15 minutes, or up to 24 hours covered.

3. Divide the mixture into 4 equal portions and shape each into a patty. Place a skillet over medium-high heat and add a drizzle of vegetable oil or 1 tablespoon (14 g) ghee. Fry each patty for 2 to 4 minutes per side. Lightly season with salt and pepper.

4. Assemble the burgers between the buns with the toppings.

Makes 4 burgers

For Patties

14 ounces (400 g) mushrooms, chopped
½ cup (110 g) canned black beans, rinsed, drained, and mashed with a fork
1 onion, quartered
¾ teaspoon salt
1 tablespoon (3 g) fresh thyme leaves
1 jarred roasted red bell pepper
1½ cups (300 g) cooked Le Puy lentils or other green lentils
2 tablespoons (30 g) tahini
2 tablespoons (30 ml) rapeseed oil
2 tablespoons (30 ml) fresh lemon juice
2 cloves garlic, crushed
1 tablespoon *pimentón* (smoked paprika)
1 tablespoon (15 ml) liquid smoke (optional)
1 tablespoon (15 ml) fresh lemon juice
¼ cup (50 g) cooked brown rice
2 tablespoons plus 1 teaspoon (5 g) fresh parsley leaves, finely chopped
2¼ teaspoons Sriracha or other hot sauce, to taste
1 teaspoon salt, plus more as needed
Freshly ground black pepper, to taste
Vegetable oil or ghee, for frying

4 buns, halved and lightly toasted

For Toppings

Sliced gherkins (pickles)
Sour cream, Greek yogurt, or vegan crème fraîche
Fresh parsley leaves
Grilled peppers (optional)

THE NORTHERNER

SMOKED TOFU | DILL | ROASTED PARSNIPS | GREEN PEA DRESSING

Dill has a powerful aroma and it's the herb and flavor most associated with Scandinavian cooking. This smoked tofu-and-dill-packed burger is reminiscent of coastal Nordic flavors. It is paired here with pungent mustard and a bright Green Pea Dressing—sauces as refreshing as the winds from the North Sea on a foggy, cold day. Top with roasted parsnips for a sweet and chunky texture.

1. Preheat the oven to 400°F (200°C).

2. To make the Green Pea Dressing: In a blender, combine all the dressing ingredients and blend until smooth. Refrigerate until it's time to assemble the burgers.

3. Place the parsnips on a rimmed baking sheet and roast for 20 minutes, or until golden, turning them halfway through the cooking time.

4. To make the patties: Place a skillet over medium-high heat and add a drizzle of rapeseed oil or 1 tablespoon (14 g) ghee. Add the onion and fry for 5 to 7 minutes until translucent. Stir in the black beans and fry for 1 to 2 minutes more, or until any excess water left from rinsing evaporates. Transfer to a large bowl.

   Add the 3 tablespoons (45 ml) rapeseed oil along with the remaining patty ingredients and mix to combine. Transfer the mixture to a food processor. Pulse for a couple of seconds until the beans break up. Be careful not to go too far—you want a crumbly texture, not a purée. Refrigerate the mixture for 15 minutes, or up to 24 hours covered.

   Divide the mixture into 4 equal portions and shape each into a patty. Place a skillet over medium-high heat and add a drizzle of rapeseed oil or 1 tablespoon (14 g) ghee. Fry the patties for 2 to 4 minutes per side. Lightly season with salt and pepper.

5. Assemble the patties between the toasted buns. Top with the mustard, Green Pea Dressing, roasted parsnips, and other toppings. Serve immediately.

Makes 4 burgers and about 2 cups (360 g) Green Pea Dressing

For Green Pea Dressing

1½ cups (195 g) frozen green peas
½ cup (75 g) pine nuts or other nut
¼ cup (60 ml) fresh lemon juice
2 tablespoons (30 ml) rapeseed oil
1 tablespoon (6 g) grated fresh ginger
¼ teaspoon salt
Water, as needed to thin the consistency

For Patties

6 to 8 parsnips, trimmed and quartered lengthwise
3 tablespoons (45 ml) rapeseed oil, plus more oil or ghee for frying
½ cup (80 g) chopped onion
1⅓ cups (298 g) drained and rinsed canned black beans, mashed with a fork
7 ounces (200 g) smoked tofu, crumbled
2 scallions, finely chopped
¼ cup (16 g) dill, finely chopped
2 tablespoons (30 ml) fresh lemon juice
¾ to 1 teaspoon salt, plus more to taste
2 tablespoons (8 g) nutritional yeast or grated Parmesan cheese
½ cup (75 g) rolled oats
Freshly ground black pepper, to taste

4 buns, halved and lightly toasted

For Toppings

4 teaspoons (16 g) mustard, divided
Sliced leek
Lettuce leaves
Cucumber slices

Recipe for Brioche Buns on page 67.

LE PARISIEN

LE PUY LENTILS | HERBES DE PROVENCE | GRUYÈRE CHEESE | APRICOT JAM

Voilà—here is a real French cheeseburger! Classic French food is synonymous with wine and herbs and this burger channels those flavors by packing powerful tarragon and subtle thyme into the patty! Nourishing lentils provide body, tangled with toasted bread crumbs, mustard, honey, and shallots. Topping with slices of Gruyère cheese gives this veggie burger that extra salty edge. Another topping that I'm extra fond of is root crisps for extra crunch. Bake your own crisps or buy them from a natural foods or organic store. I love a mix of beet and sweet potato or potato crisps in my burgers.

1. Preheat the oven to 425°F (220°C).

2. To make the patties: Place a skillet over medium-high heat and add a drizzle of olive oil or 1 tablespoon (14 g) ghee. Add the shallots and Herbes de Provence. Fry for about 5 minutes until the shallots are soft and translucent. Transfer to a large bowl and add the remaining patty ingredients (through bread crumbs). Use your hands to combine the mixture until a sticky texture forms.

   Taste and adjust the seasonings with more salt and pepper if needed. Refrigerate the mixture for 15 minutes, or up to 24 hours covered.

3. Divide the mixture into 4 equal portions and shape each into a patty. Place the patties on a rimmed baking sheet and bake for 15 to 18 minutes. Carefully flip them about halfway through the cooking time.

4. Three to 4 minutes before they are done, top each patty with a slice of Gruyère. Assemble the patties between the buns and top with the additional toppings.

Makes 4 burgers

For Patties

Olive oil or ghee, for frying

4½ ounces (130 g) shallots, thinly sliced into rounds

1 tablespoon (3 g) Herbes de Provence

2 cups (400 g) cooked Le Puy lentils or other firm green lentils

¼ cup (50 g) cooked brown rice

2 cloves garlic, crushed

2 tablespoons (5 g) finely chopped fresh thyme leaves

1 tablespoon (15 ml) red wine vinegar

¾ teaspoon salt, plus more to taste

¼ teaspoon freshly ground black pepper, plus more to taste

1 tablespoon (11 g) mustard

1 teaspoon honey or packed brown sugar

⅓ cup (40 g) toasted bread crumbs, or a scant ⅔ cup (40 g) panko bread crumbs

4 slices Gruyère cheese

4 buns, halved and lightly toasted

For Toppings

Caramelized Onions (page 32)

Apricot jam or confit (or other sweet marmalade or jam)

Mayonnaise or vegan mayonnaise (page 152)

Root Crisps (page 138; optional)

JUST RAW ONION

RAW ONION | CITRUS ZEST

I wouldn't be so cheeky as to add a recipe for raw onion here, but I want to say a few words about this natural-ly pungent topping. Put your effort into cutting them for maximum deli-ciousness. It's all about texture. Slice your rounds very thin and, for dicing, go for tiny dices. A tip: To soften the pungency of raw onion, soak the onion for 20 minutes in ice-cold water, then rinse and drain.

Raw onion topping is beautiful in its simplicity, but if you like to get creative and make it special, add ½ teaspoon lemon or lime zest and 1 tablespoon finely chopped herbs per serving for a fresh taste. Plan on 1 tablespoon (8 g) diced raw onion per serving or a medium-sized onion for 4 burgers.

PICKLED ONION

RED ONION | APPLE CIDER VINEGAR

This vibrant pink topping makes your burger look irresistible. Pick-led onions add a sassy sweet-and-sour finish that's a perfect counter-point for savory and spicy burgers. Omit the syrup or sugar if you are on a sugar-free diet, but that wee bit of sweetening makes the pickle extra delicious.

1 medium-sized red onion, thinly sliced
½ cup (120 ml) apple cider vinegar
1 tablespoon (20 g) agave syrup or sugar
½ teaspoon salt, plus more to taste

In a large glass bowl stir together all the ingredients. This will keep refrigerated in sealed jars for 3 to 4 days.

Makes about 2¾ to 3½ ounces, or 80 to 100 g (8 to 10 servings)

ALTERNATIVE PICKLING

Use rice vinegar, instead of apple cider vinegar and coconut sugar instead of agave or syrup.

CRISPY SHALLOTS

SHALLOT | OLIVE OIL

Adding crispy shallots to a burger, especially one that is a softer patty, perfects the bite. This basic recipe in-volves just shallots and vegetable oil, but you can take it to that next level by tossing the shallots in rice flour before frying to add extra crispness. Use any onion you prefer here.

Olive oil, for frying
1 small shallot per serving, thinly sliced into rounds
1 tablespoon (10 g) rice flour per serving (optional)

Toss the shallots in the rice flour (if using) and shake to remove any excess. Place a skillet over medium-high heat and add some olive oil. Fry the shallots for 8 to 10 minutes until golden but not burned, stirring to avoid burning. Remove from the skillet with a slotted spoon and place on a paper towel to cool.

Yield varies based on how many shallots you used

Caramelized Onions,
recipe on page 32

CARAMELIZED ONIONS

GHEE | ONION | APPLE CIDER VINEGAR

When onions are heated and slowly cooked in fat, magic happens. Slow heating releases the natural sweetness and a sticky caramel deliciousness in the onions. The idea is to stir continuously to avoid crispness—the onions should cook in their own juices and butter or oil. I choose ghee or olive oil for the best taste, though coconut and rapeseed oil are good too.

While the onions produce their own sweetness, you can intensify the result by adding a little sugar, cider, or wine. For a Nordic flavor palate, I'm using apple cider vinegar here. You could use beer instead for that extra acid juiciness. To give the onions a French spin, use red or white wine.

¼ cup (50 g) ghee, coconut oil, or vegetable oil
7 ounces (200 g) thinly sliced onions
1 to 2 tablespoons (9 to 18 g) coconut sugar or (15 to 30 g) packed brown sugar (optional)
6 tablespoons plus 2 teaspoons (100 ml) apple cider vinegar (Or use red or white wine vinegar, balsamic vinegar, red wine, cider, or beer.)
1 teaspoon dried thyme (optional)

Heat a large skillet over medium-high heat and add 3 tablespoons (42 g) ghee (add the remaining ghee while cooking to avoid burning). Stir in the onions and sugar (if using) and cook for 6 to 7 minutes, stirring. Add the vinegar and thyme (if using), stirring, and let the onions cook and reduce in the juices until the liquids are absorbed fully. Remove from the heat and let cool.

Makes about 5 ounces (150 g)

APPLE AND FENNEL SLAW

FENNEL | APPLE | CABBAGE | YOGURT | MAYONNAISE

The Netherlands is famous for crowd-pleasing food such as pancakes, cheese, and bread! But more importantly, the Dutch have gifted the world the perfect burger companion—coleslaw! Or as it's called in Dutch "koolsla," meaning cabbage salad! Cabbage, a cruciferous vegetable, is a timeless superfood, dense with vitamins and fiber and low in calories. What's not to love about it? This slaw is made light and fresh with fennel, which adds a light anise taste, perfectly harmonizing with the sweet apple. For the tastiest slaw texture, shred or slice the ingredients very finely.

3 tablespoons plus 1 teaspoon (50 g) natural or plant-based yogurt
3 tablespoons plus 1½ teaspoons (50 g) mayonnaise or vegan mayonnaise
2 tablespoons (30 ml) apple cider vinegar
2 tablespoons (30 ml) fresh lemon juice
1 tablespoon (15 g) Dijon mustard
½ teaspoon honey or agave syrup
Drizzle of extra-virgin olive oil
½ teaspoon salt, plus more as needed
¼ teaspoon freshly ground black pepper, plus more as needed
2 fennel bulbs, thinly sliced
3 scant cups (200 g) thinly shredded green cabbage
1 apple, thinly sliced (choose a sweet, firm one such as Pink Lady)
3 tablespoons (12 g) finely chopped fresh parsley leaves

1. In a small bowl, stir together the liquid ingredients and the salt and pepper.

2. In a large bowl, combine the fennel, cabbage, apple, and parsley. Pour in the sauce, stir to combine, taste, and adjust the seasonings with more salt and pepper if needed. Serve immediately or refrigerate until needed.

Makes about 1 quart (700 g)

DUTCH SEAPORT BURGER

ROASTED CAULIFLOWER | SEAWEED | KALE | GOUDA | APPLE AND FENNEL SLAW

When salty winds and rain pour in over the lands, the Dutch take comfort in fuss-free food with lots of flavor. Cauliflower is a popular vegetable in the Netherlands as it adds a subtle mustardy taste to simple dishes. Eating cauliflower is a good health investment as it's proven to increase heart health and block and prevent cancerous cell growth. This cauliflower patty is enriched with salty seaweed and topped with the famous Gouda cheese (vegans can substitute a vegan cheese) and finished with a refreshing crispy apple and fennel slaw.

1. To make the patties: Preheat the oven to 410°F (210°C). Place the cauliflower on a rimmed baking sheet and sprinkle with salt. Roast for 30 minutes, or until crispy, turning halfway through the cooking time.

2. Place a skillet over medium-low heat and add a drizzle of oil or 1 tablespoon (14 g) ghee. Add the onion and fry for 3 to 4 minutes until translucent. Add the kale and garlic. Fry for 3 to 4 minutes more, stirring. Remove from the heat.

3. Transfer the roasted cauliflower to a food processor and pulse for a few seconds until it has a crumbly texture. Add the onion and kale and pulse for a few seconds more. Transfer the mixture to a large bowl. Add the remaining patty ingredients, season to taste with salt and pepper, and mix to combine. Refrigerate the mixture for 30 minutes uncovered, or up to 24 hours covered.

   Divide the mixture into 4 equal portions. Shape each into a patty. In a skillet over medium-high heat, fry the patties for 3 to 4 minutes per side, or until nicely browned. Top each with a slice of cheese at the end of frying. Remove from the pan when the cheese melts.

4. Serve with bread, if desired, and topped with the slaw.

Makes 4 burgers

For Patties

17½ ounces (500 g) cauliflower florets

1 teaspoon salt

2 tablespoons (30 ml) rapeseed oil or 2 tablespoons (28 g) ghee, plus more for frying

2½ ounces (70 g) finely sliced onion

3½ ounces (100 g) kale, stemmed, finely chopped

1 clove garlic, crushed

1 scant cup (20 g) soaked, rinsed, and finely chopped hijiki or dulse (Or use fresh herbs or alliums, such as chives or scallions.)

5 tablespoons (20 g) fresh dill, chopped

6 tablespoons plus 2 teaspoons (50 g) oat flour

½ cup (100 g) cooked brown rice or barley

½ cup (30 g) fresh parsley leaves, chopped

2 tablespoons (8 g) nutritional yeast or grated Parmesan cheese

2 tablespoons (30 ml) fresh lemon juice

Salt and freshly ground black pepper, to taste

4 slices mature Gouda cheese, vegan cheese, or other cheese of choice

4 buns, halved and lightly toasted

For Topping

Apple and Fennel Slaw (page 32)

A fried egg makes
an extra-scrumptious
veggie burger topping.

'SHROOM AND EGG BURGER

MUSHROOMS | BARLEY | MUSTARD | MAYONNAISE | FRIED EGG

This scrumptiously comforting burger is inspired by British pub food, which is generally recognized for its down-to-earth, no-fuss cooking style. The barley patties are extra filling and flavored with condiment sauces, spices, and mushrooms. Mustard, mayonnaise, and a sunny-side up fried egg tie the flavors together in this very satisfying and proper veggie burger!

1. To make the black bean patties: Preheat the oven to 140°F (60°C). Place a skillet over medium-high heat and add the oil. Add the mushrooms and fry for 7 to 8 minutes, stirring, or until fragrant and shriveled. Transfer to a large bowl and combine with the remaining patty ingredients (through agave). Use your hands to work the mixture into a good texture that holds together well. Taste and season with salt and pepper. Refrigerate the mixture for 15 minutes, or up to 24 hours covered.

2. To make the mustard mayo: In a small bowl, whisk the mayonnaise and mustard until smooth. Sprinkle with chives and set aside.

3. Divide the mushroom–black bean mixture into 4 equal portions and form each into a patty. Place a skillet over medium-high heat and fry the patties for 3 to 4 minutes per side, or until nicely browned. Keep the patties warm in the oven while frying the eggs to your desired doneness.

4. Assemble the burgers between the buns and top each with a fried egg and Mustard Mayo.

Makes 4 burgers and about ⅓ cup (90 g) Mustard Mayo

TIP!
Don't like mushrooms? Use onions in the patties anywhere where mushrooms are called for.

MUSHROOMS
Fried Mushrooms are scrumptious as toppings and add plenty of umami flavor to patties. Fry mushrooms in batches to avoid overlapping the pieces in the pan. Overlap creates mushiness. Clean mushrooms with a little brush rather than washing them under water as they absorb liquid like sponges! Alternatively, peel the mushrooms instead of washing the skins, but be aware that with peeling you also lose nutrition stored in the mushroom skin.

For Patties
Drizzle of vegetable oil or 1 tablespoon (14 g) ghee
About 5¾ cups (400 g) roughly chopped mushrooms
1⅓ cups (298 g) drained and rinsed canned black beans, mashed with a fork
1½ scant cups (70 g) panko bread crumbs
2 tablespoons (30 ml) soy sauce or tamari
1 tablespoon (15 g) Sriracha
2 cloves garlic, crushed
½ scant cup (70 g) cooked barley or other whole grain
3 tablespoons (9 g) finely chopped fresh chives
2 tablespoons (8 g) fresh parsley leaves, finely minced
1 teaspoon *pimentón* (smoked paprika)
Salt and freshly ground black pepper, to taste

4 buns, halved and lightly toasted

For Mustard Mayo
⅓ cup (75 g) mayonnaise or vegan mayonnaise (page 152)
1 tablespoon (15 g) mustard, Dijon or English
Finely chopped chives, for garnishing

For Toppings
4 small organic eggs
Pickled Onion (page 30)
Fried mushrooms
Tomatoes
Chopped chives

BERLINER BURGER

LEEK | LENTILS | BLACK BEANS | PINK KRAUT | CURRY KETCHUP

Inspired by old-school Berlin kiosk foods, this modern burger is topped with both kraut and curry ketchup—two iconic German street foods. The curry ketchup is the most popular ketchup in Germany and it is delicious with burgers and as a dipping sauce for roasted wedges and strips. The basic black bean burger is enhanced with leek, chives, and parsley. The quick pink kraut needs to be made in advance (up to two weeks) or at least half an hour before starting to cook the burgers.

1. To make the patties: Place a large skillet over medium-high heat and add a drizzle of vegetable oil. Add the onion and fry for 5 to 7 minutes until soft and translucent. Add the garlic and mushrooms. Fry until the mushrooms shrivel and the excess moisture evaporates. Add the leek and fry for another minute. Transfer to a bowl and combine with the remaining patty ingredients.

2. Use a fork or your hands to make a sticky mixture, or pulse lightly in batches in the food processor. Taste and adjust the seasonings with salt and pepper if needed. Transfer the mixture to a bowl and refrigerate for 15 minutes, or up to 24 hours covered.

3. Divide the mixture into 4 equal portions and shape each into a patty. Place a skillet over medium-high heat and add a drizzle of vegetable oil or 1 tablespoon (14 g) ghee. Fry the patties for 3 to 4 minutes per side. Lightly season with salt and pepper.

4. Assemble the patties in the toasted buns and top with mayonnaise, kraut, and Curry Ketchup.

Makes 4 burgers

For Patties

Vegetable oil or ghee, for frying

1 medium onion, finely chopped

2 cloves garlic, crushed

7 ounces (200 g) mushrooms, finely chopped

1 cup (100 g) finely sliced leek

1¼ (250 g) cooked and drained dark lentils

½ cup (100 g) roasted and ground sunflower seeds or other ground nuts

1 tablespoon (11 g) mustard

2 tablespoons (8 g) nutritional yeast or grated Parmesan cheese (optional)

1 (15 g) chili paste

2 tablespoons (30 ml) white vinegar

⅔ cup (30 g) panko or regular bread crumbs

¾ teaspoon salt, plus more to taste

¼ teaspoon freshly ground black pepper, plus more to taste

4 buns, halved and lightly toasted

For Toppings

Mayonnaise or vegan mayonnaise (page 152)

Curry Ketchup (page 42)

Pink Kraut (page 42)

PINK KRAUT

CABBAGE |
APPLE CIDER VINEGAR |
RED ONION

Cabbage is full of valuable nutrition and it's an inexpensive staple food. Making kraut is one brilliant way of using it in everyday cooking. Kraut is one of the most traditional and well-known German dishes. This pink version makes a big batch so you can make use of a whole cabbage head. The kraut keeps for 2 weeks in the refrigerator—use it generously on burgers and any savory food that calls for sour toppings.

Vegetable oil or 1 tablespoon (14 g) ghee
1 small (about 2 to 3 pounds, or 800 g to 1 kg) red or green cabbage, thinly sliced
1¼ cups (300 ml) water, plus more as needed
1 cup plus 2 teaspoons (250 ml) apple cider vinegar
1 tablespoon (18 g) salt
1 red onion, finely sliced

Place a saucepan over medium-high heat and add a drizzle of vegetable oil. Add the remaining ingredients and stir to combine. Cover and cook for 30 minutes, checking frequently that the bottom of the kraut is not burning. Add a little more water if needed. Set aside and let it cool. Transfer to a storage container and keep refrigerated between servings.

Makes about 2½ pounds (1.2 kg)

CURRY KETCHUP

TAMARIND | GARAM MASALA |
KETCHUP

Germans love curry ketchup, and for a good reason. Curry makes ketchup extra interesting. Use this sauce on the Berliner Burger (page 41) and anywhere else you use regular ketchup.

1 tablespoon (15 ml) rapeseed oil or (14 g) coconut oil
1 tablespoon garam masala
2 teaspoons tamarind paste or (10 ml) Worcestershire sauce
1 teaspoon ground cumin
1 teaspoon chili powder
1 teaspoon coconut sugar or sweetener of choice
1 cup (240 g) Homemade Ketchup (page 47) or your favorite store-bought brand

Place a small saucepan over medium heat and add the oil. Stir in the garam masala, tamarind paste, cumin, chili powder, and coconut sugar. Cook for 1 minute, stirring. Stir in the ketchup until combined. Let simmer for 1 minute. Remove from the heat and let cool. Transfer to a storage container and refrigerate.

Makes about 1 cup (about 240 g)

FRITJE OORLOG

POTATO | SATAY SAUCE |
MAYONNAISE

This is a classic Dutch side dish in the Amsterdam street kitchens. Fritje Oorlog means "war fries" in Dutch, which makes no sense to me because it's the most perfect union of flavors. Satay sauce (peanut sauce) and mayonnaise and onion are heavenly to serve with baked or fried potatoes.

14 ounces (400 g) potatoes, peeled and cut in wedges
Salt
Olive oil
½ cup (100 ml) Satay Sauce (page 120)
½ cup (100 g) mayonnaise or vegan mayonnaise (page 152)
⅓ cup (50 g) chopped raw onions

1. Preheat the oven to 425°F (220°C). Place the potato wedges on an oven tray, and sprinkle with salt and drizzle with olive oil.

2. Bake in the oven until the potatoes are golden and baked through, around 20 to 25 minutes. Serve with Satay Sauce and mayonnaise.

Makes 4 servings and about 1 cup (250 g) sauce

SPICY HERB AND BROAD BEAN BURGER

DILL | BROAD BEANS | GRILLED VEGETABLES | ROOT CRISPS | CARAMELIZED ONIONS

This recipe is loosely inspired by the broad bean burger served by Burger-meester in Amsterdam, a regular meat burger restaurant that also serves veggie burgers that are truly delicious! The restaurant version of this burger is favored by Middle Eastern spices and herbs. But I like to mix my broad beans with Nordic leek and dill—an interesting combination with cilantro and a good match with Lemon Mayonnaise.

1. For the Lemon Mayonnaise: Mix the mayonnaise ingredients together. Cover and place in the fridge until serving.

2. For the patties: Place a saucepan over medium-high heat and add a drizzle of vegetable oil. Fry the onion until transparent. Add the leek and fry for another minute.

3. Combine the patty ingredients in a bowl. Refrigerate the mixture for 15 minutes, or up to 24 hours covered.

4. Divide the mixture into 4 equal portions and shape each into a patty. Place a skillet over medium-high heat and add a drizzle of vegetable oil or 1 tablespoon (14 g) ghee. Fry the patties for 3 to 4 minutes per side. Lightly season with salt and pepper.

5. Layer the toppings with the patties between the buns. Serve with the Root Crisps.

Makes 4 burgers and about ½ cup (100 g) Lemon Mayonnaise

For Lemon Mayonnaise
½ cups (100 g) mayonnaise or vegan mayonnaise (page 152)
Zest of ½ lemon

For Patties
Vegetable oil or ghee, for frying
1 onion, sliced
⅓ scant cup (30 g) white part of the leek, chopped small
⅓ scant cup (40 g) toasted cashews, ground to fine crumbles
1 cup (298 g) drained and rinsed canned broad beans, mashed with a fork
4 tablespoons (16 g) finely chopped fresh dill
3 tablespoons (3 g) finely chopped fresh cilantro
½ tablespoon (8 ml) olive oil
2 tablespoons (8 g) finely chopped fresh parsley
1 flaxseed or chia egg (page 14)
2 cloves garlic, crushed
4 cups (200 g) panko or regular bread crumbs
3 tablespoons (12 g) nutritional yeast or grated Parmesan cheese
1 tablespoon (15 ml) hot sauce, such as Sriracha
¾ teaspoon salt, plus more to taste
¼ teaspoon freshly ground black pepper
1 teaspoon freshly grated ginger

4 buns, halved and lightly toasted
Root Crisps (page 138)

For Toppings
Caramelized Onions (page 32)
Grilled vegetables, such as eggplant and peppers
Tomato and fresh cucumber

HOMEMADE KETCHUP

TOMATOES | CELERY | COCONUT SUGAR | RED WINE VINEGAR

Everyone's favorite childhood condiment, ketchup, has been on health foodies' black lists for decades, mainly due to its high sugar content and long list of additives found on the ingredients labels of popular brands. Bring ketchup back into the warmth of your kitchen by making your own delicious version from scratch! Don't be put off by the amount of coconut sugar in this recipe—you are only supposed to have a squeeze on your burger, so it's just a small part of your whole meal.

1. Place a saucepan over medium-high heat and add a drizzle of olive oil. Add the red onion and celery and fry for about 2 minutes until softened and fragrant. Add the garlic, spices, and hot sauce. Cook, stirring for 1 to 2 minutes, before adding the fresh and canned tomatoes, capers, and water. Cook for 15 minutes. Remove from the heat and pour the sauce through a sieve twice to make it smooth.

2. Return the sauce to the saucepan and stir in the vinegar, Worcestershire sauce, and coconut sugar. Let the sauce simmer and reduce to your desired thickness. Remove from the heat and bottle the ketchup when cooled. Refrigerate.

Makes 1 quart (1 L)

Olive oil, for frying
1 red onion, finely chopped
1 cup (100 g) finely chopped celery
2 cloves garlic, crushed
1 teaspoon ground coriander
¼ teaspoon ground cinnamon
½ teaspoon cumin seeds
½ teaspoon mustard seeds
½ teaspoon fennel seeds
1 teaspoon salt
½ teaspoon freshly ground black
   pepper
⅓ teaspoon hot sauce
1¾ pounds (800 g) best-quality plum
   tomatoes, chopped small
1 can (14 ounces, or 400 g)
   plum tomatoes
2 tablespoons capers
6 tablespoons plus 2 teaspoons
   (100 ml) water
6 tablespoons plus 2 teaspoons
   (100 ml) red wine vinegar
1 tablespoon Worcestershire sauce
¼ cup (40 g) coconut sugar or
   2 tablespoons plus 2 teaspoons
   (40 g) packed brown sugar

SMÖRGÅS BURGER

BEET TARTAR | HORSERADISH SOUR CREAM | ROOT CRISPS | AVOCADO

Swedes often like to eat red beet salad on their breads, and we call breads with toppings a smörgås. This is a smörgås burger featuring a cold beet and quinoa tartar patty topped with a peppery horseradish cream. The twist here is the avocado used in place of bread. Though avocado is not a traditional Scandinavian ingredient, it's a perfect fit with the cool Nordic flavors. You can serve the beet tartar patty on regular bread too, of course.

1. To make the Horseradish Sour Cream: Mix the ingredients together, cover, and place in the fridge until assembly.

2. To make the patties: Combine the patty ingredients in a bowl. Shape 4 patties and place them on a tray. Cover with plastic, and refrigerate for 15 minutes or up to 24 hours.

3. Slice the rounding on an avocado half's backside so that it will stand stable on a flat surface. Top with a beet tartar patty and toppings. Top with a second avocado half if you like a top bun, or enjoy it as a smörgås—open.

Makes 4 burgers

For Horseradish Sour Cream
6¾ fluid ounces (200 ml) crème fraîche, Greek yogurt, sour cream, or vegan yogurt-crème fraîche
3 tablespoons (50 ml) freshly grated horseradish (adjust strength after tasting)
1 teaspoon lemon juice
Salt, to taste

For Patties
9 ounces (250 g) cooked and peeled beets, finely chopped
3 ounces (75 g) red quinoa, cooked and drained
1 teaspoon honey or agave syrup
½ cup (75 g) goat cheese, feta cheese, or vegan cheese, in fine crumbles
Salt and freshly ground black pepper, to taste
1 teaspoon extra-virgin olive oil
2–3 scallions, chopped finely

2–4 avocados, halved lengthwise and pitted

For Toppings
Pickled Onion (page 30)
Fresh green salad
Horseradish Sour Cream
Root Crisps (page 138)
Fresh lemon wedges
Sprouts (I used beet sprouts.)

SUPER GOOD QUINOA SPELT BUNS

SPELT FLOUR | QUINOA FLAKES | EGGS OR AQUAFABA | FLAXSEEDS

When I first made these buns I couldn't believe how good they tasted after adding quinoa flakes! Spelt flour is my flour of choice. The dough isn't as flexible as regular wheat flour dough (due to its lesser gluten content), but it makes up for it with a satisfying nutty flavor. Adding quinoa gives these buns an extra protein boost. This is an extra-nourishing burger bun and you can make it vegan by replacing the egg with 3 tablespoons (45 ml) aquafaba. Aquafaba is the water that has been used to cook chickpeas in. You can use the liquid from a can of cooked chickpeas.

1. In a small saucepan over medium heat, heat the water until hot. Remove from the heat and let cool to 98°F (37°C).

2. Transfer to a small bowl and stir in the agave syrup and yeast. Let the yeast rest in the liquid for 5 minutes, or until frothy.

3. Combine the water-yeast mixture with oil and egg.

4. Combine the flour, quinoa flakes, and salt in a bowl.

5. Pour the liquid into the flour mix and combine into a sticky dough.

6. Dust the working surface with flour and knead the dough for about 10 minutes until smooth. Place the dough in a clean bowl, cover, and let rise for 1½ to 2 hours.

7. When the dough has risen in size, punch it down and knead it for a few minutes. Use more flour to dust if needed. Divide the dough into 12 to 18 balls, depending on how large you want your buns. Place the buns on a baking sheet, cover, and let rest for another hour.

8. Preheat the oven to 400°F (200°C). Brush the buns with the egg white mixed with a little water, or brush with olive oil for the glaze. Sprinkle with the sesame seeds. Bake in the middle of the oven for 15 minutes, or until golden brown and sounding hollow when you knock on the surface. Let cool before serving.

Makes 12 to 18 buns

1½ cups (350 ml) water

2 tablespoons (40 g) agave syrup, honey, or maple syrup

1 package (2¼ teaspoons, or 7 g) active dry yeast

3 tablespoons plus 1 teaspoon (50 ml) vegetable oil

1 large egg, room temperature (lightly beaten) or 3 tablespoons (45 ml) aquafaba

3½ cups (438 g) spelt flour

1 cup (102 g) quinoa flakes

1 teaspoon salt

1 egg white (lightly beaten) or olive oil, for glazing

Sesame seeds or flaxseeds, for topping

SOUTHERN EUROPE

The Mediterranean kitchen is famous for its sun-kissed,
delicious food. The Mediterranean diet is considered
one of the healthiest in the world, usually low in
saturated fats and high in fiber and vitamins, so
it's well worth taking inspiration from.

Garlic, olives, and tomatoes are ingredients that shine in
food from the south of France, Spain, Italy, and Greece.
The warmer climate also produces an abundance of vibrant
produce such as zucchini, eggplant, peppers, citrus, grapes,
basil, and a wealth of fruit. The flavors of southern
Europe are often described as simple and sophisticated
at the same time—something never out of style.

MARS BURGER

ROMANESCO | PARMESAN CHEESE | MINT | CHIOGGIA BEET

Veggie burgers have the ability to come in all the colors of the rainbow and this emerald burger gets its vibrant color from a funky-looking vegetable— Romanesco, which originates from Italy and is a close relative to broccoli and cauliflower. You'll recognize it by its stunning fractal appearance. It's milder and nuttier in taste than cauliflower and has plenty of superfood qualities, such as being high in vitamins, iron, and fiber, making it a superb choice for your weekday meals.

All brassicas, when used in patties, need a little extra support for binding. The bread crumbs and Parmesan cheese help it stick together. I often make my own fresh bread crumbs by toasting thinly sliced bread really dry, and crumbling it by hand.

Just like broccoli, Romanesco needs only a few basic additions to shine, such as garlic, lemon zest, and Parmesan for perfect harmony. The patty is topped with another supernatural-looking Italian vegetable, the Chioggia beet (optional).

1. Preheat the oven to 425°F (220°C).

2. To make the patties: In a food processor, pulse the Romanesco into a crumbly rice-like texture. With your hand, squeeze out the excess moisture from the Romanesco crumble over your sink, using a sieve with your other hand underneath to catch any falling crumble. Transfer to a large bowl and add the remaining patty ingredients (through bread crumbs) and use your hands to combine. Taste and adjust the seasonings with salt and pepper if needed. Add a little more bread crumbs if you like a firmer hold. Refrigerate for 15 minutes, or up to 24 hours covered.

3. Divide the mixture into 4 equal portions and shape each into a patty. Lightly season with salt and pepper. Place the patties on a rimmed baking sheet and bake for 20 minutes. Watch the patties during the last 5 minutes to avoid burning.

4. Serve on the toasted buns topped with the dressing, avocado, tomatoes, and beet (if using).

Makes 4 burgers

For Patties

14 ounces (400 g) Romanesco florets
  (or bimi or broccolini)
2 to 3 cloves garlic, or to taste, crushed
¾ teaspoon salt, plus more to taste
¼ teaspoon freshly ground
  black pepper
2½ tablespoons (10 g) fresh mint
  leaves, finely chopped
1 red or green chile pepper, seeded and
  finely chopped
½ cup (50 g) grated Parmesan cheese
  or Rawmesan (page 58), or 1 cup
  (60 g) nutritional yeast
1 cup (50 g) panko or regular bread
  crumbs, plus more as needed

4 rustic spelt buns, halved and
  lightly toasted

For Toppings

New Caesar Dressing (page 58)
Avocado slices
Cherry tomatoes, sliced
1 Chioggia beet, peeled and cut into
  matchsticks (optional)

TIP!
Use gluten-free bread crumbs.
Make them yourself by toasting
and crumbling gluten-free bread.

NEW CAESAR DRESSING

NUTS | CAPERS | GARLIC | MUSTARD

The world's most famous lunch salad is based on its iconic sauce—Caesar dressing! This burger dressing is egg- and fish-free, and you can substitute nutritional yeast for the Parmesan cheese if you want to veganize it! To create the salty flavors typically provided by the anchovies, I'm adding pine nuts and garlic, with support from piquant capers! In a time when more people want to enjoy healthy meals without cutting down on flavor, this new style of Caesar dressing is here to stay!

½ cup (60 g) toasted cashew nuts
2 tablespoons plus 1 teaspoon (20 g)
    pine nuts
2 tablespoons (8 g) nutritional yeast or
    grated Parmesan cheese
2 tablespoons (30 ml) olive oil
1 tablespoon (15 ml) fresh lemon juice
2 cloves garlic
1 teaspoon mustard
1 teaspoon capers
Water, to thin the consistency

In a blender, blend all ingredients to your desired consistency. Transfer to a sealed jar or other small container and keep refrigerated for 3 to 4 days.

Makes about 5 fluid ounces (150 ml)

TIP!
This sauce is delicious on salads and breads. Make a big batch to keep in the fridge and enjoy with different meals throughout the week.

RAWMESAN

PINE NUTS | NUTRITIONAL YEAST | GARLIC

When there's a will there's a way! Rawmesan doesn't taste exactly like grated Parmesan cheese but it does have a similar addictive cheesy quality. Rich with umami from nutritional yeast flakes and nuts, this vegan and gluten-free topping can be used just like Parmesan, in and on top of all sorts of foods.

¾ cup (100 g) pine nuts or other
    lightly toasted nuts
5 tablespoons (19 g)
    nutritional yeast
1 clove garlic, crushed

In a food processor, combine the ingredients and pulse until a crumbly texture forms. Refrigerate in an airtight container for up to 1 week.

Makes about 5 ounces (150 g)

GREEK BURGER

MINT | ZUCCHINI | FETA CHEESE

This delicious burger is inspired by the popular Greek snack *kolokithokeftedes*—a zucchini fritter that's hard to pronounce but easy to love. Fresh, juicy, and savory at the same time. Feta adds a salty edge and scallions lend a mild onion flavor. Zucchini has plenty of moisture so for patties that stay together squeeze some out before cooking. Use a baking ring to keep the burgers in perfect shape.

1. To make the Vegan Feta Cream (if using): In a food processor or blender, combine all the ingredients, season to taste with salt and pepper, and pulse into a crumby texture.

2. To make the patties: Preheat the oven to 140°F (60°C). Squeeze as much liquid from your zucchini as you can over a sieve or fold it into a cheesecloth and squeeze. Place the drained zucchini in a large bowl and combine with the remaining patty ingredients. Season to taste with salt and pepper.

   Divide the mixture into 4 equal portions and shape each into a patty. Place a large skillet over medium-high heat and add a drizzle of vegetable oil or 1 tablespoon (14 g) ghee. Fry the patties for 3 to 4 minutes per side, or until nicely browned.

3. To make the Creamy Chili Dressing: In a small bowl, stir together the mayonnaise, red pepper flakes, and lime juice.

4. Assemble the burgers on the buns and serve topped with the Creamy Chili Dressing.

Makes 4 burgers, about ½ cup (90 g) Vegan Feta Cream, and about ¾ cup (200 g) Creamy Chili Dressing

For Vegan Feta Cream
2¾ ounces (80 g) soaked cashews
2 tablespoons (8 g) nutritional yeast
1 tablespoon plus 2 teaspoons (25 ml) extra-virgin olive oil
Juice of ½ of a lemon
Salt and freshly ground black pepper, to taste

For Patties
2 zucchini, roughly grated
6 scallions, finely chopped
2 eggs, beaten, or 2 chia eggs (page 14)
3½ ounces (100 g) feta cheese, finely crumbled, or Vegan Feta Cream
3 cloves garlic, crushed
1½ scant cups (70 g) panko or regular bread crumbs
1¼ cups (150 ml) chickpea flour or other flour of choice
Salt and freshly ground black pepper, to taste
Vegetable oil or ghee, for frying

4 buns, halved and lightly toasted

For Creamy Chili Dressing
1 scant cup (200 g) mayonnaise, crème fraîche, or vegan cashew cream
1 teaspoon red pepper flakes
Juice of 1 lime or lemon

TIP!
This patty is delicious with a number of sauces and toppings. Try Kalamata Tapenade (page 63), Romesco Sauce (page 63), Lime Zhug (page 87), or Dill and Mustard Cashew Sauce (page 152) for variation.

SWEET POTATO WEDGES

SWEET POTATOES

Wedges are the perfect side dish to burgers. These finger-licking-good sweet potato wedges are delicious with dip sauces like Romesco Sauce or Kalamata Tapenade (see right), or a garlic sauce like the Cashew Toum (page 92).

17½ ounces (500 g) sweet potatoes, peeled and cut into wedges
Thyme, paprika, and rosemary, to taste
Drizzle of olive oil
Salt and freshly ground black pepper, to taste

1. Preheat the oven to 400°F (200°C). In a large bowl, toss the wedges with the thyme, paprika, rosemary, and olive oil. Season to taste with salt and pepper.

2. Divide the wedges between 2 rimmed baking sheets. Bake for 30 minutes, turning the wedges about halfway through the roasting time. Serve warm with Romesco Sauce or your favorite dips.

Serves 4, as a side

TIP!
Dust the wedges with spices. Try cinnamon, red pepper flakes, nutritional yeast, Ras El Hanout, *pimentón* (smoked paprika), or other favorites.

The white sauce in the image is a Cashew Toum sauce, which is a garlic sauce reminiscent of aioli. For the recipe, see page 92.

ROMESCO SAUCE

ALMONDS |
ROASTED RED BELL PEPPER

If you visit Spain, you will notice that romesco sauce is traditional on restaurant and café menus. This versatile flavor-packed sauce is made with toasted almonds, bell pepper, *pimentón* (smoked paprika), and bread crumbs. Utterly delicious!

2½ ounces (75 g) toasted almonds
2½ ounces (75 g) toasted bread crumbs
3 tablespoons (47 g) tomato purée
2 cloves garlic, peeled
1 jarred roasted red bell pepper
1 tablespoon (15 ml) sherry vinegar
1 teaspoon *pimentón* (smoked paprika)
1 teaspoon salt
Pinch red pepper flakes
¼ cup plus 2 teaspoons (70 ml) olive oil

In a food processor, combine all the ingredients, *except* the olive oil, and blend until combined. Slowly pour the olive oil into the mixture and blend until smooth. Transfer to an airtight container and refrigerate. It will keep for 2 to 3 days.

Makes 13½ fluid ounces (400 ml)

KALAMATA TAPENADE

KALAMATA OLIVES | CAPERS

Tapenade is a delicious spread and topping! This recipe uses black olives, but you can also use green. When olives are harvested young they are green, and as they grow ripe they turn black. Olives are an essential ingredient in the south of Europe, adding rich aromatic salt-iness to meals. Tapenade is a paste of finely chopped olives with capers. You can use it to top burgers or add to patty mixtures.

2 cups (200 g) pitted and finely chopped black olives
2 tablespoons (18 g) capers
2 cloves garlic, crushed
6 tablespoons (100 ml) olive oil

Blend the tapenade ingredients together in a food processor for a few seconds. Store sealed in the refrigerator until serving. Keeps in the refrigerator for a week.

Makes about 1½ cups (350 ml)

NIÇOISE BURGER

ROASTED BEETS | HONEY | CHÈVRE | WALNUTS

Chèvre is one of the star ingredients from the kitchens in the south of France. It pairs beautifully with the sweetness of roasted beets. These burgers are also lovely topped with Walnut Pistou (page 73).

1. Preheat the oven to 400°F (200°C). In a medium-sized bowl, toss the beet slices with olive oil and sprinkle with salt, pepper, and thyme. Place the beet slices on a rimmed baking sheet and bake for 30 to 35 minutes until cooked through, flipping about halfway through the cooking time. During the last 5 minutes of cooking, top the beet slices with slices of chèvre.

2. Assemble the patties on the French bread. Top with the walnuts and arugula. *Bon appétit!*

Makes 4 burgers

For Patties

2 large red beets, peeled and sliced
    about ½-inch (1 cm) thick
Olive oil, for cooking
Salt and freshly ground black pepper,
    to taste
1 tablespoon (3 g) fresh thyme leaves
2 teaspoons (14 g) honey or agave syrup
3½ ounces (100 g) fresh chèvre or soft
    vegan cheese

4 pieces French bread, halved

For Toppings

Chopped walnuts
2½ cups (50 g) arugula

CLASSIC BRIOCHE BUNS

FLOUR | EGGS | SESAME SEEDS

You can use a variety of bread for your burgers, but when you are looking for a reliable and winning concept, classic brioche is the burger bun favored by most. Light and with a thin crust, it's especially suited to veggie burgers, which can be overpowered by heavier bread. If you want a funky color, try adding a tablespoon of charcoal powder for a black bun or spirulina for a green bun.

1. In a small saucepan over medium heat, heat the milk until hot. Remove from the heat and let cool to 98.6°F (37°C). Transfer to a small bowl and stir in the sugar and yeast. Let the yeast rest in the liquid for 5 minutes, or until frothy.

2. Mix in the beaten eggs and salt.

3. In a large bowl, combine the flour, the charcoal or spirulina powder (if using), and the butter. Use your fingertips to work the butter into the flour until you have a fine crumbly texture. Make a well in the middle and add the egg and yeast mixture. Work the dough to combine the ingredients into a sticky dough.

   Alternatively, use a food processor to work the butter into the dough. Add the egg and yeast mixture and process until a sticky dough forms.

4. Dust the working surface with flour and knead the dough for about 10 minutes until smooth. Place the dough in a clean bowl, cover, and let rise for 1½ to 2 hours.

5. When the dough doubles in size, punch it down and knead it for a few minutes. Use more flour to dust if needed. Divide the dough into 12 to 18 balls, depending on how large you want your buns. Place the buns on a baking sheet, cover, and let rest for another hour.

6. Preheat the oven to 425°F (220°C). Brush the buns with the egg yolk mixed with a little water and sprinkle with the sesame seeds. Bake in the middle of the oven for 15 minutes, or until golden brown. Let cool before serving.

Makes 12 large buns or 18 slider buns

1 cup plus 3 tablespoons (280 ml) nut milk or cow's milk

1 tablespoon (13 g) sugar

2¼ teaspoons dry yeast

2 organic eggs, beaten

Pinch salt

17½ ounces (500 g) bread flour (avoid soft flours used for cakes), plus more for dusting

1 tablespoon (3 g) charcoal or spirulina powder (optional)

4 tablespoons (56 g) butter, at room temperature

1 organic egg yolk

Sesame seeds, for sprinkling

CAPRESE BURGER

SUN-DRIED TOMATOES |TOMATO PISTOU | BASIL | BURRATA

This burger celebrates classic Italian flavors. Its mouthwatering combination of tomato, garlic, balsamic vinegar, and herbs will make you think of classic Bolognese sauce and meatballs. Top with fresh basil and Burrata cheese for a creamy, cool contrast! *Mangia!*

1. To make the patties: Place a skillet over medium-high heat and add a drizzle of olive oil or 1 tablespoon (14 g) ghee. Add the onion and fry for 6 to 7 minutes until translucent. Transfer to a bowl.

2. Return the skillet to the heat and add more olive oil. Fry the mushrooms until golden and shriveled. Transfer to the bowl with the onion and add the remaining patty ingredients.

3. In batches, pulse the patty mixture in a food processor into a rough and crumbly texture with visible pieces. Divide the mixture into 4 equal portions and shape each into a patty.

4. Place a skillet over medium-high heat and add a drizzle of olive oil. Fry the patties for 3 to 4 minutes per side, or until nicely browned.

5. Assemble on the toasted buns and serve topped with Burrata, basil, balsamic, and tomato slices.

Makes 4 burgers

For Patties

Olive oil or ghee, for frying

1 onion, finely sliced 9 ounces (250 g) mushrooms, chopped

1 cup (50 g) soaked and drained sun-dried tomatoes, finely chopped

1 cup (200 g) cooked dark lentils

1 tablespoon (15 ml) olive oil

1 tablespoon (2 g) fresh marjoram leaves

1 tablespoon (15 ml) balsamic or red wine vinegar

1 teaspoon agave syrup or honey

2 cloves garlic

¾ cup plus 1 tablespoon (50 g) nutritional yeast or ½ cup (50 g) Parmesan cheese

1½ scant cups (70 g) panko or regular bread crumbs

½ scant cup (70 g) cooked farro or brown rice

½ scant cup (20 g) finely chopped basil

Salt and freshly ground black pepper, to taste

4 buns, such as pieces of ciabatta bread or use portobello mushrooms as buns

For Toppings

Burrata or other soft Italian cheese, or vegan cheese

Fresh basil leaves

Balsamic vinegar

Tomato Pistou (page 73)

Fresh tomato slices

PORTOBELLO BURGER

PORTOBELLO MUSHROOM | SWEET POTATO | WALNUT PISTOU

Possibly the simplest burger in the book—and incredibly tasty—with the portobello mushrooms serving as buns. Vegan and gluten free.

1. Place a skillet over medium-high heat and add a drizzle of olive oil. Fry the red bell pepper slices for 3 to 4 minutes. Set aside until assembly.

2. Return the skillet to the heat and add another drizzle of olive oil. Place 2 portobello mushrooms in the skillet and fry for 1 minute per side. Sprinkle with a pinch of salt and reduce the heat to medium-low. Cover the skillet and steam the mushrooms for about 2 minutes, turning twice. Remove from the heat.

3. Increase the heat to medium-high and add another drizzle of olive oil. Place 2 sweet potato slices in the pan and sprinkle with red pepper flakes and salt. Fry for 3 to 5 minutes total, turning, until nicely done.

4. Build the burger using the mushrooms as buns and layering with sweet potato, red bell pepper, avocado, spinach, onions, pistou, and Lemony Cashew Cream. Enjoy!

Makes 4 burgers

For Patties

Olive oil or ghee, for frying
1 red bell pepper, sliced into rounds
8 portobello mushrooms, stemmed
Salt and freshly ground black pepper, to taste
8 sweet potato slices (rounds), about 1 inch (30 mm) thick
Red pepper flakes, for seasoning

For Toppings

1 avocado, sliced into rounds
1 bunch fresh baby spinach or arugula
Caramelized Onions (page 32)
Walnut Pistou (page 73)
Lemony Cashew Cream (page 142)

WALNUT PISTOU

BASIL | WALNUTS | PARMESAN CHEESE | EXTRA-VIRGIN OLIVE OIL

Pesto is a wonderful invention—finely chopping fresh herbs to release their powerful aromas enhanced by olive oil and salt is pure genius. A simple yet flavorful pesto can be made with a minimum of ingredients. But adding nuts, garlic, and lemon juice elevates the pesto to another level. Here, walnuts are featured with basil. A great add-in for both pastas and sauces and a perfect topping for Italian- and French-inspired burgers.

1 large bunch fresh basil leaves
3½ ounces (100 g) walnuts or pine nuts
¼ cup (60 ml) extra-virgin olive oil
2 tablespoons (10 g) grated Parmesan cheese or nutritional yeast
1½ teaspoons fresh lemon juice, plus more as needed
Salt, to taste

In a food processor, combine all the ingredients and blend until smooth. Taste and adjust the seasonings with more salt or lemon juice if needed. Transfer to an airtight container and refrigerate.

Makes about 5 ounces (150 g)

CILANTRO PISTOU

CILANTRO | CASHEWS | WALNUTS

Fresh cilantro combined with garlic, chili, basil, and roasted nuts is a dreamy topping on breads and burgers.

3½ ounces (100 g) walnuts or pine nuts
1 clove garlic
1 bunch fresh cilantro
1 bunch fresh basil
3½ ounces (100 g) roasted cashew nuts (optional)
¼ cup (60 ml) extra-virgin olive oil
1 tablespoon (15 ml) toasted sesame oil (optional)
2 tablespoons (10 g) grated Parmesan cheese or nutritional yeast
1½ teaspoons fresh lemon juice (optional)
Pinch of red pepper flakes (optional)
Salt, to taste

1. In a food processor, combine all the ingredients and blend until smooth.

2. Taste and adjust the seasonings with more red pepper flakes or salt if needed.

3. Transfer to an airtight container and refrigerate.

Makes about 1 cup (300 g)

TOMATO PISTOU

SUN-DRIED TOMATO | GARLIC

Sun-dried tomatoes are a powerful and nutritious flavor maker. Use this beautiful red pesto as a topping or in patty mixtures for extra good flavor.

A big handful of sun-dried tomatoes presoaked for 30 minutes and drained
1 large bunch fresh basil leaves
1 clove garlic
¼ cup (60 ml) extra-virgin olive oil
3½ ounces (100 g) or pine nuts (optional)
1½ teaspoons red or balsamic vinegar
½ teaspoon salt, or more to taste

1. In a food processor, combine all the ingredients and blend until smooth.

2. Taste and adjust the seasonings, adding more balsamic vinegar or salt if needed.

3. Transfer to an airtight container and refrigerate.

Makes about 5 ounces (150 g)

SUNSHINE BURGER

CARROT | BUCKWHEAT| FETA | LEMON | RED CABBAGE KIMCHI

This burger marries salty feta cheese with lemon and the sweetness of carrots through poppy buckwheat! It's a refreshing veggie burger. The flavors are typical of Greek and southern European dishes, topped with buttery avocado slices and spicy kimchi for a hot highlight. The deep purple color of this kimchi is achieved by using red cabbage instead of Asian cabbage. Smother with a garlic mayonnaise for a creamy finish.

1. To make Garlic Mayonnaise: Mix the ingredients in a bowl and set aside until assembly.

2. To make the patties: Combine the patty ingredients in a bowl. In batches, pulse the patty mixture in a food processor into a rough and crumbly texture with visible pieces. Or alternatively, use a fork or your hands to make a sticky texture. Divide the mixture into 4 equal portions and shape each into a patty. Leave the mixture covered in the fridge for 30 minutes or up to 24 hours.

3. Place a skillet over medium-high heat and add a drizzle of olive oil. Fry the patties for 2 to 4 minutes per side, or until nicely browned.

4. Assemble on the toasted buns and serve topped with avocado, Garlic Mayonnaise, and Kimchi.

Makes 4 burgers

For Garlic Mayonnaise
½ scant cup (100 g) mayonnaise
1 teaspoon freshly grated garlic
Salt, to taste

For Patties
Olive oil or ghee, for frying
1¾ ounces (50 g) feta cheese
1 cup (100 g) roughly grated carrot
½ cup plus 1 tablespoon (100 g) cooked buckwheat
3 scallions, finely chopped
1 tablespoon (15 ml) fresh lemon juice
Handful of fresh delicate herbs such as coriander, parsley, and mint, finely chopped
Salt and freshly ground black pepper, to taste

4 buns, halved and lightly toasted

For Toppings
Avocado slices
Garlic Mayonnaise
Kimchi (page 110) or Pink Kraut (page 42)

TIP!
This burger is delicious with a variety of toppings and sauces such as Kalamata Tapenade (page 63), New Caesar Dressing (page 58), or Avocado Lime Cream (page 132). You can substitute fresh micro sprouts for the kimchi for a fresher, less spicy bite.

THE MIDDLE EAST & NORTH AFRICA

There is an abundance of vibrant, bold flavors in the food from the Middle East and North Africa. Typically, dishes from the region balance spicy, earthy flavors with tangy citrus and herbs.

The most significant ingredients are spices: Saffron, cinnamon, cloves, coriander, and cumin all add delicious character to dishes. Other common staples include olives, nuts, peppers, tahini, dates, parsley, mint, chickpeas, and pomegranates. Popular grains are rice, freekeh, wheat bulgur, and couscous.

Following is a buffet of burgers inspired by these exciting flavors.

LACHMACUN BURGER

LE PUY LENTILS | CILANTRO | CASHEW TOUM | HARISSA

The flavors of this burger are inspired by Turkish and Armenian pizzas known as lachmacun. Though traditionally a meat dish, the tastiness of lachmacun lies in the contrast between the peppery hot spices and the cool salad and garlicky Cashew Toum sauce. Lentils flavored by cinnamon, cumin, and coriander make a delicious patty. Finish with crispy lettuce, onion, and sauces.

1. To make the patties: Preheat the oven to 140°F (60°C). Heat a large skillet over medium-high heat and add a drizzle of olive oil or 1 tablespoon (14 g) ghee. Add the mushrooms and fry for 7 to 8 minutes, or until they have shriveled and any excess liquid has cooked away. Add the garlic and fry for 1 minute more.

2. Stir in the lentils, harissa, cumin, salt, and cinnamon. Fry for 3 to 4 minutes, or until fragrant and any excess liquid has cooked away.

3. Mix in the walnuts, bulgur, cilantro, and sun-dried tomatoes. Transfer the mixture to a food processor in batches and pulse until you have a rough crumbly texture with bits and pieces left. Refrigerate the mixture for 15 minutes, or up to 24 hours covered.

   Divide the mixture into 4 equal portions and shape each into a small patty. In a skillet over medium-high heat, fry the patties for 2 to 3 minutes per side, or until nicely browned. Lightly season with pepper and more salt, to taste. Place the patties on a rimmed baking sheet and bake for 8 to 10 minutes.

4. Assemble the patties in the Turkish bread and top with toum, red onion, lettuce, mint, and cilantro.

Makes 4 burgers

For Patties

Olive oil or ghee, for frying
2¾ cups (193 g) mushrooms, chopped
3 cloves garlic, crushed
1½ cups (250 g) cooked Le Puy lentils
   or other dark lentils
2 tablespoons (30 g) Homemade
   Harissa (page 94) or store-bought
1 teaspoon ground cumin
¾ teaspoon salt, plus more to taste
Pinch ground cinnamon
3½ ounces (100 g) walnuts, lightly
   toasted and ground
¼ cup (50 g) cooked bulgur or
   brown rice
1 scant cup (15 g) fresh cilantro leaves,
   finely chopped
1 scant cup (50 g) sun-dried tomatoes,
   soaked, drained, and puréed
Freshly ground black pepper, to taste

4 buns, halved and lightly toasted

For Toppings

Cashew Toum (page 92)
Red onion slices
Finely shredded iceberg lettuce
Handful fresh mint leaves,
   finely chopped
Handful fresh cilantro leaves,
   finely chopped

SAFFRON FREEKEH BURGER

SAFFRON | SWEET POTATO | GREEN TAHINI DRESSING

This irresistible burger combines Halloumi, freekeh, and harissa! Freekeh is not as known and popular outside the Middle East as its fellow grains, couscous and bulgur, though it deserves all your attention because of its wonderful roasted flavor. Drizzle the Green Tahini Dressing over for a powerful taste experience.

1. To make the Saffron Mayonnaise: When your mayonnaise ingredients are at room temperature, whip the egg yolk and vinegar with mustard, saffron, and a little salt in a bowl. Add the oil and keep whipping, starting with drops and then adding more generously. Taste and adjust with salt and vinegar if needed.

2. To make the patties: Place a skillet over medium-high heat and add a drizzle of vegetable oil. Quickly fry the freekeh until fragrant. Pour in the water. Bring to a boil, reduce the heat to low, and let it simmer for 15 minutes. Add more water if needed. Remove from the heat and set aside to cool.

3. Place another skillet over medium-high heat and add a drizzle of vegetable oil or 1 tablespoon (14 g) ghee. Add the onion and fry for 5 to 7 minutes until soft and translucent. Transfer to a large bowl.

4. Add the freekeh to the bowl, along with the remaining patty ingredients through the salt, and stir to combine. Transfer to a food processor and pulse into a crumbly texture. Taste and adjust the seasonings with pepper and more salt if needed. Refrigerate for 15 minutes, or up to 24 hours covered.

5. Place a skillet over medium-high heat and add a drizzle of vegetable oil or 1 tablespoon (14 g) ghee. Fry the patties for 3 to 4 minutes per side. Lightly season with salt. Layer the Saffron Mayonnaise as a base on bottom bun half, and serve topped with the Green Tahini Dressing, cilantro, pistachios, and avocado slices.

Makes 4 burgers

For Saffron Mayonnaise

1 egg yolk
1 tablespoon (15 ml) white
   wine vinegar
1 tablespoon (11 g) mustard
½ teaspoon saffron
Salt
5 fluid ounces (150 ml) mild olive oil

For Patties

Vegetable oil or ghee, for frying
¼ cup plus 1 tablespoon (50 g)
   uncooked cracked or
   whole-grain freekeh
¾ cup (175 ml) water
1 onion, finely chopped
3½ ounces (100 g) sweet potato,
   peeled and diced small
2 cloves garlic, crushed
2 tablespoons (30 g) Homemade
   Harissa (page 94) or store-bought
1 tablespoon (15 ml) fresh lemon juice
1 tablespoon (15 ml) olive oil
¾ teaspoon salt, plus more to taste
Freshly ground black pepper, to taste

4 buns, halved and lightly toasted

For Toppings

Green Tahini Dressing (page 87)
Fresh cilantro leaves
Chopped pistachio nuts
Avocado slices
Fresh lime juice

KASBAH BURGER

EGGPLANT | MUSHROOM | FREEKEH | HARISSA

With hints of cinnamon, pistachio, and sweet raisins, this eggplant burger is a snapshot of the everyday flavors of North African cuisine. Dressed with a delicious pepper and walnut sauce from Syria, *muhammara*, its sure to be a crowd pleaser!

1. Preheat the oven to 350°F (180°C). Place the mushrooms, eggplant, and red onion on a rimmed baking sheet and sprinkle with salt and pepper. Bake for 30 minutes. Let cool. Transfer the cooked vegetables to a large bowl and add the remaining ingredients (through cinnamon) and mix to combine. Transfer to a food processor and pulse for few seconds until the mixture is sticky. Refrigerate the mixture for 15 minutes, or up to 24 hours covered.

2. Place a skillet over medium-high heat and add a drizzle of vegetable oil or 1 tablespoon (14 g) ghee. Fry the patties for 3 to 4 minutes per side. Lightly season again with salt and pepper. Place the patties on a rimmed baking sheet and bake for 8 to 10 minutes.

3. Serve the patties between the warm buns topped with the Muhammara.

Makes 4 burgers

For Patties
2¾ cups (193 g) mushrooms
1 small eggplant, halved
1 medium-sized red onion, thinly sliced
1 teaspoon salt
Freshly ground black pepper, to taste
1 cup (228 g) cooked freekeh or bulgur
½ cup (78 g) rolled oats
3 cloves garlic, crushed
3 tablespoons (27 g) pistachios, ground
2 tablespoons (18 g) raisins, finely chopped
2 tablespoons (8 g) nutritional yeast or grated Parmesan cheese
1 tablespoon (15 g) Homemade Harissa (page 94) or store-bought
1 teaspoon *pimentón* (smoked paprika)
1 teaspoon ground cinnamon
Vegetable oil or ghee, for frying

4 buns, halved and warmed

For Toppings
Muhammara (page 92)
Thinly shredded red cabbage
Fried or baked sweet potato slices
Avocado

FALAFEL

CHICKPEAS | HARISSA | FETA CREAM

Falafels are common Middle Eastern street food. Made from protein-rich chickpeas, that wonderfully versatile legume that also serves as the basis for hummus. Traditionally, falafel is deep-fried but here we panfry and oven bake it for a fresher, healthier bite. These falafels need to be handled carefully as they break easily. Serve these with a dab of harissa and fresh herbs. They are perfect as a starter for 10 people, or serve 2 each as a more filling meal.

1. Preheat the oven to 350°F (180°C).

2. To make the falafel: In a food processor, combine all the falafel ingredients (through salt). Blend the ingredients carefully into a crumbly texture. Refrigerate the mixture for 15 minutes, or up to 24 hours covered.

3. Divide the mixture into 20 equal portions and shape each into a small ball. Place a skillet over medium-high heat and add a drizzle of olive oil. Fry until nicely browned, about 1 to 2 minutes per side. Lightly season with salt and pepper. Transfer to a rimmed baking sheet and bake for 8 to 10 minutes.

4. Serve in the pitas topped with Feta Cream, harissa, red onion, and mint.

Makes 20 small falafel balls or 8 burgers

For Falafel

⅔ cup (10 g) fresh cilantro leaves, finely chopped

1⅓ cups (312 g) drained and rinsed canned chickpeas, mashed with a fork

½ cup (100 g) cooked brown rice or freekeh

1 small red onion, finely diced

6 tablespoons plus 2 teaspoons (50 g) chickpea flour

3 cloves garlic

1½ teaspoons ground cumin

1 tablespoon (15 ml) olive oil, plus more for frying

1 teaspoon salt, plus more to taste

Freshly ground black pepper, to taste

10 small whole-grain pitas

For Toppings

Feta Cream or Vegan Feta Cream (page 87)

Homemade Harissa (page 94) or store-bought

Red onion slices

Fresh mint or parsley leaves

GREEN TAHINI DRESSING

TAHINI | LEMON JUICE | PARSLEY | GARLIC

This is possibly my absolute favorite cold sauce—it's packed with incredible flavor, mixing sweet and sour, with pungent garlic and the Moorish nutty tahini! This sauce can adorn any burger in this chapter, and you can also add it to salads, roasted vegetables, and warm dishes that need that little extra flavor spark. Make double batches and enjoy later in the week. Add 1 teaspoon chlorella powder for an extra healthy boost.

2 tablespoons (30 g) white tahini (regular brown tahini is just as tasty but gives a less vibrant green color)
Juice of 1 lemon (Use a lime for an even tangier taste.)
Generous handful fresh parsley or other delicate herbs, such as mint or basil
2 cloves garlic, crushed
Salt, to taste
2 tablespoons (30 ml) water
1 teaspoon chlorella (optional)
½ teaspoon honey

In a blender or food processor, combine all the ingredients and blend into a smooth sauce. Transfer to an airtight container and refrigerate for up to 2 days.

Makes about 4 fluid ounces (120 ml)

FETA CREAM & VEGAN FETA CREAM

FETA CHEESE | CRÈME FRAÎCHE

Salty with a tangy creaminess, this cheesy cream is the perfect burger topping, or use anywhere you want a sauce with a cold, rich edge! For a vegan alternative, make a cashew fraîche with nutritional yeast.

For Feta Cream
1¾ ounces (50 g) feta cheese
⅓ cup (75 g) Greek yogurt
Salt and freshly ground black pepper, to taste

For Vegan Feta Cream
2½ ounces (75 g) Lemony Cashew Cream (page 142)
2 tablespoons (8 g) nutritional yeast
Salt and freshly ground black pepper, to taste
2 tablespoons (30 ml) extra-virgin olive oil
Juice of ½ lemon

In a food processor or blender, combine all the ingredients for your cream of choice. Blend together. Transfer to an airtight container and refrigerator for up to 2 days.

Makes about 4½ ounces (125 g) Feta Cream and about 3½ ounces (100 g) Vegan Feta Cream

LIME ZHUG

CILANTRO | LIME JUICE | GARLIC

Zhug is a spicy cilantro sauce originating from Yemen. It is basically the Middle Eastern version of salsa verde, combining fresh herbs with tangy citrus.

3 cups plus 2 tablespoons (50 g) fresh cilantro leaves
¾ cup plus 1 tablespoon (50 g) fresh parsley leaves
1 green bell pepper, stemmed
2 cloves garlic, crushed
3 tablespoons (45 ml) extra-virgin olive oil
Juice of 1 lime
Salt and freshly ground black pepper, to taste

In a food processor, combine all the ingredients and blend until smooth. Transfer to an airtight container and refrigerate for up to 1 week.

Makes 5⅓ ounces (150 g)

HABIBI BURGER

BROCCOLI | WHITE BEANS | SCALLIONS | CASHEW TOUM

There's plenty of green goodness going on in this recipe. Broccoli and white beans make a juicy, green, nourishing patty and the zesty herb-packed Lime Zhug (page 87) and Cashew Toum (page 92) make for an interesting finish!

1. To make the patties: Preheat the oven to 425°F (220°C). Combine the patty ingredients (through the harissa) in a large bowl. Taste and adjust to your liking with salt and pepper. Transfer the mixture to a food processor and pulse for a few seconds into a crumbly texture. Refrigerate the mixture for 15 minutes, or up to 24 hours covered.

2. Lightly season again with salt and pepper. Divide the mixture into 4 equal portions and shape each into a patty. Place on a rimmed baking sheet and bake for 20 minutes.

3. Assemble the patties on the buns and spread with Cashew Toum.

Makes 4 burgers

For Patties

7 ounces (200 g) steamed broccoli, very finely chopped

5 scallions, finely chopped

6 tablespoons (25 g) fresh mint leaves, finely chopped

¼ cup plus 2 tablespoons (25 g) fresh parsley leaves, finely chopped

About 1¼ cups (320 g) drained and rinsed canned white beans, mashed with a fork

2 tablespoons (8 g) nutritional yeast or grated Parmesan cheese

2 cloves garlic, crushed

1 tablespoon (15 g) tahini

1 tablespoon (15 ml) olive oil

¾ teaspoon salt

1 teaspoon green harissa, red harissa, or other chili sauce

Salt and freshly ground black pepper, to taste

4 buns, halved and lightly toasted

4 tablespoons (60 ml) Cashew Toum (page 92)

For Toppings

Lime Zhug (page 87)

2 carrots, julienned

GRILLED HALLOUMI BURGER

HALLOUMI | RED PEPPER HUMMUS | MINT-ONION SLAW

Salty Halloumi, fresh mint slaw, and creamy red pepper hummus capture the Cypriot flavors in this well-rounded burger. Halloumi, a delicious, salty, firm cheese originating from Cyprus, is made from goat's and sheep's milk and holds its shape in high temperatures, making it perfect to grill and fry. The Greek and Cypriot corner of Europe, near Turkey, is a melting pot for Mediterranean and Middle Eastern flavors. I combine the best of these two worlds in this scrumptious burger. Vegans can grill firm tofu instead of Halloumi.

1. To make the Spicy Cilantro Dressing: In a blender or food processor, combine all the dressing ingredients. Process until you have a smooth sauce.

2. To make the Mint-Onion Slaw: In a large bowl, stir all the slaw ingredients together until combined and set aside.

3. To make the patties: In a grill pan or skillet over medium-high heat, fry the Halloumi slices for 1 to 2 minutes per side until golden.

   Assemble the burgers on the buns: Spread the buns with the dressing, layer on some slaw, and top with the Halloumi and Red Pepper Hummus.

Makes 4 burgers

For Spicy Cilantro Dressing

6¾ fluid ounces (200 ml) cashew cream, silky tofu, or crème fraîche

1 scant cup (15 g) fresh cilantro leaves

1 green chile pepper, seeded and finely chopped

1 tablespoon (15 ml) fresh lemon juice

½ teaspoon ground cumin

¼ teaspoon salt

For Mint-Onion Slaw

4½ cups (300 g) finely shredded green cabbage, or sturdy green leaves

1 red onion, finely sliced

4 tablespoons plus 1½ teaspoons (30 g) fresh mint leaves, finely chopped

¼ cup (56 g) mayonnaise or vegan mayonnaise

Juice of ½ lemon

Drizzle of extra-virgin olive oil

Salt and freshly ground black pepper, to taste

For Patties

1 (about 9 ounces, or 250 g) piece Halloumi cheese, sliced into 4 flat pieces

4 buns, halved and lightly toasted

For Toppings

Red Pepper Hummus (page 92)

RED PEPPER HUMMUS

ROASTED RED PEPPER | CHICKPEAS | TAHINI | LEMON

Hummus—that perfect blend of chickpeas, lemon, and tahini—has become one of the most popular dips in the world. This version is flavored with roasted red peppers, giving it a juicy, peppery taste. Hummus is easy to customize: For a classic hummus, omit the red pepper or substitute fresh cilantro and lime for a fresh and tangy taste.

1 can (14 ounces, or 400 g) chickpeas, drained and rinsed
1 jarred roasted red bell pepper or 2 tablespoons (30 g) Homemade Harissa (page 94)
3 cloves garlic, crushed
3 tablespoons plus 1 teaspoon (50 ml) fresh lemon juice, plus more to taste
3 tablespoons (45 g) tahini
¾ teaspoon salt, plus more to taste
Water, to thin the consistency

In a blender or food processer, combine all the ingredients, *except* the water, and process until smooth. Add water to thin the hummus to your desired consistency. Taste and adjust the seasonings with more lemon juice or salt if needed.

Makes about 1 pound (454 g)

MUHAMMARA

ALEPPO AND BELL PEPPERS | POMEGRANATE SEEDS | WALNUTS

It's easy to forget, amidst the war reports, that Syria, before the war, was a place of culinary delights and the birthplace of a truly delicious dip sauce—muhammara!

1 cup (120 g) chopped toasted walnuts
1 jarred roasted red bell pepper
3 tablespoons (21 g) toasted bread crumbs, plus more as needed
3 tablespoons plus 1 teaspoon (50 ml) extra-virgin olive oil, plus more as needed
1 tablespoon (15 ml) fresh lemon juice
1 tablespoon (28 g) pomegranate seeds
1 teaspoon ground cumin
1 teaspoon salt, plus more to taste
1 teaspoon Aleppo pepper flakes
1 clove garlic, crushed

In a food processor or blender, combine all the ingredients and blend into a smooth dip. Adjust the consistency by adding more olive oil for a smoother dip or more bread crumbs for thickness. Taste and adjust the salt. Refrigerate the sauce in an airtight container or jar for 3 to 4 days.

Makes 14 ounces (400 g)

CASHEW TOUM

GARLIC | LEMON | CASHEWS

A real garlic hit! The Middle Eastern version of aioli—toum! My version swaps some of the olive oil for cashew cream, and it's delicious!

1 whole head garlic, peeled
1½ teaspoons salt, plus more as needed
Juice of 1 lemon, plus more as needed
3½ ounces (100 g) cashews, soaked for 1 to 3 hours in enough water to cover and drained
6 tablespoons plus 2 teaspoons (100 ml) extra-virgin olive oil

1. In a blender or food processor, combine the garlic, salt, and lemon juice. Process until puréed.

2. Add the soaked cashews and blend until smooth.

3. Add a small bit of water if it's too dry. Taste and adjust with more lemon juice and salt if needed. Refrigerate in an airtight container or jar where it will keep for 3 to 4 days.

Makes 5 to 7 ounces (150 to 200 g)

HOMEMADE HARISSA

GARLIC | ALEPPO CHILE PEPPERS | CUMIN | ROASTED RED BELL PEPPER

Tunisian harissa is a popular chili sauce used throughout the Middle East, and it's been embraced by foodies all over the world, making it easy to find in Western supermarkets too. Nothing beats the flavors of a homemade version, though. By taking time to slowly fry the spices, chiles, and onions, you'll be rewarded with the most mouthwatering aromas from your kitchen. Use this harissa as a chili sauce with burgers in this chapter or anywhere you would otherwise use chili sauce—add it to hummus, soups, breads, and stews.

1. Place a skillet over medium-high heat and add a drizzle of olive oil or 1 table-spoon (14 g) ghee. Add the red onion, garlic, and chiles. Fry for 10 minutes, stirring. Reduce the heat if they start to burn.

2. In a small dry skillet over medium-high heat, combine the cumin, coriander, and caraway seeds. Toast for 3 to 4 minutes until fragrant. Grind the toasted spices with a mortar and pestle or in a clean spice blender until finely ground. Transfer to a blender or food processor

3. Add the cooked onion, garlic, and chiles to the spices, along with the tomato purée, lemon juice, roasted red pepper, and salt. Process until smooth. Taste and add more salt if needed. Transfer to a sealable jar and refrigerate. It will keep for up to 2 weeks.

Makes about 8½ fluid ounces (250 ml)

3 tablespoons plus 1 teaspoon (50 ml) olive oil, plus more olive oil or ghee, for frying

1 red onion, finely sliced

5 cloves garlic, crushed

4 or 5 Aleppo chiles or other red hot chile peppers

2 teaspoons (4 g) cumin seeds

2 teaspoons (4 g) coriander seeds

1 teaspoon caraway seeds

1 teaspoon tomato purée

Juice of 1 lemon

1 roasted red bell pepper, chopped

1 teaspoon salt, plus more to taste

TIP!
Visit Morrocan or Asian speciality shops or natural food shops for the best-quality tahini and olive oils.

A SWEET DATE AND RASPBERRY TREAT

MEDJOOL DATES | MIXED NUTS | RASPBERRY

Raw, or no-bake, cakes are all the rage these days and this vegan treat is both delicious and safe to eat for gluten- and dairy-sensitive eaters. This dessert is inspired by ice cream s'mores and raw Oreo cakes. It is incredibly easy to make: blend, knead, cut out, chill, and assemble! Vary the filling flavors by substituting other berries or fruit for the raspberries.

1. To make the Date and Nut Cookies: In a food processor, combine all the cookie ingredients and process into a sticky mixture.

2. Turn the dough out onto a work surface and place it between 2 sheets of parchment paper. Press it out to about ¼-inch (6 mm) thick between the parchment sheets. Use a round cookie cutter about 1½ inches (3.5 cm) to cut out 8 cookies. Refrigerate the cookies for 2 hours.

3. To make the Raspberry Cream: In a blender or food processor, combine all the ingredients, and blend into a smooth cream. Cover and refrigerate until assembly, or freeze for 30 minutes for an ice cream–like version.

4. Remove the cookies from the fridge and spoon the raspberry filling onto 1 cookie. Place another cookie on top and press the cookies together to make the filling stick. Repeat with the remaining cookies and raspberry cream. Serve straight away.

Makes 4 filled cookies

For Date and Nut Cookies

5 ounces (150 g) Medjool dates, soaked for 1 hour in enough water to cover and drained

About ¾ cup (100 g) mixed roasted nuts (pistachios, almonds, walnuts, and cashews)

2 tablespoons (10 g) cacao powder

2 tablespoons (28 g) coconut oil, melted, or olive oil

1 teaspoon vanilla extract

¼ teaspoon ground cardamom

Pinch salt

For Raspberry Cream

5¼ ounces (150 g) soaked cashews, drained

3½ ounces (100 g) raspberries

About 3 tablespoons (40 g) coconut butter, melted (optional)

2 tablespoons plus 2 teaspoons (40 ml) agave syrup

1 teaspoon orange zest

Pinch salt

Crimson colored Beet Crisps
(see recipe for Root Crisps
on page 138)

ASIA

With an abundance of flavors and broad range of cooking styles, Asia is a land full of good food inspiration. Rice is its most popular grain and is widely used throughout Asia. Other typical ingredients are ginger, garlic, sesame seeds, soy, and chiles, making the basis for the most alluring curries and stir-fries in the world! Asia is also the home of tofu and tempeh, both great ingredients for making enticing burger patties.

In Southeast Asia, particularly India, Malaysia, and Indonesia, it's common to use coconut, fresh cilantro (also called coriander), tamarind, and lemongrass to make comforting curries. Thai, Chinese, and Vietnamese cuisines excel in tangy soy sauces and vibrant wok dishes. And don't forget the refreshing, invigorating flavors of Japan—a wasabi hit, anyone? Asian food is never dull!

BBQ EGGPLANT NOODLE BURGER

EGGPLANT | ASIAN BBQ SAUCE | PORTOBELLO MUSHROOM

These delectable grilled eggplant burgers are slathered with a scrumptious Asian BBQ sauce. Charred eggplant is a wonderful base for spicier sauces. To make it even more interesting, serve them with Rainbow Noodle Slaw (page 104). You can also just add grated carrot and cucumber shavings with a drizzle of rice vinegar if you are in a rush. Here I use portobello mushrooms as buns because they pair beautifully with the eggplant, but you can use regular brioche or other bread of your choice.

1. To make the patties: Place a grill pan over medium-high heat and add a drizzle of vegetable oil. Sprinkle the eggplant slices with salt and fry them for 7 to 8 minutes per side. Transfer the slices to a plate.

2. To make the Asian BBQ Sauce: Heat a saucepan over medium-high heat and add a drizzle of vegetable oil. Fry the banana shallots with the star anise for 8 to 10 minutes until the shallots start to caramelize. Stir in the remaining BBQ sauce ingredients, reduce the heat to low, and let simmer for 7 to 8 minutes. Remove and discard the star anise.

3. Add the eggplant slices to the sauce and simmer for 2 to 3 minutes. Turn off the heat.

4. Place a skillet over medium-high heat, add a drizzle of vegetable oil. Add the portobello mushrooms—it's best to do this in batches. Fry for 1 minute per side and place a lid on the pan. Let the mushrooms steam for 3 minutes. Remove the lid and let cool. Pat any excess moisture from the mushrooms with a paper towel.

5. Serve immediately: Place the eggplant between the portobellos and layer on the mayo and Rainbow Noodle Slaw.

Makes 4 burgers and about 6¾ fluid ounces (200 ml) Asian BBQ sauce

For Patties
Vegetable oil, for frying
2 small Asian eggplant or 1 medium-sized regular eggplant, cut into 12 rounds about ½ inch (1 cm) thick
Salt, to taste
8 portobello mushrooms

For Asian BBQ Sauce
Vegetable oil, for frying
2 banana shallots or 1 large red onion, finely sliced
1 star anise
2 cups plus 1½ tablespoons (500 ml) vegetable broth
6 tablespoons plus 2 teaspoons (100 ml) Hoisin Sauce (page 104)
3 tablespoons plus 1 teaspoon (50 ml) soy sauce or tamari
3 tablespoons (60 g) honey or agave syrup
3 tablespoons (45 g) Homemade Ketchup (page 47)
2 tablespoons plus 2 teaspoons (40 ml) water
2 cloves garlic, crushed
1 tablespoon (15 g) Sriracha
1 tablespoon (15 ml) rice vinegar
1 tablespoon (6 g) grated fresh ginger

For Toppings
Rainbow Noodle Slaw (page 104)
Mayonnaise (page 152)

RAINBOW NOODLE SLAW

BOK CHOY | CARROT | FENNEL | SOBA NOODLES

This bold and colorful coleslaw is a little extra cheeky—mixing aromatic fennel ribbons with gluten-free soba noodles, fresh carrot, and bok choy all covered in a sour plum vinegar dressing. If you cannot get bok choy, use chard, fresh spinach, or leafy greens. Ume plum vinegar is made from the leftover brine of pickled Japanese plums. It is sour and salty with a fruity character.

For Dressing

2 tablespoons (30 ml) toasted sesame oil
3 tablespoons (45 ml) ume plum or red wine vinegar
1 tablespoon (15 ml) soy sauce or tamari
½ teaspoon honey or agave syrup
2 tablespoons (28 g) mayonnaise or vegan mayonnaise
Sesame seeds, for garnishing

For Slaw

1 small red onion, thinly sliced
1 carrot, julienned or grated
1 fennel bulb, shaved into thin shreds
1 bok choy, finely chopped
2½ ounces (70 g) cooked soba noodles or glass noodles, drained and chilled (optional)

1. To make the dressing: In a small bowl, stir together all the dressing ingredients and a sprinkle of sesame seeds. Set aside.

2. To make the slaw: In a large bowl, combine all the slaw ingredients (through soba noodles). Pour the dressing over and toss to coat. Cover and refrigerate until serving.

Makes 14 to 18 ounces (400 to 500 g) depending on the weight of the vegetables

VIETNAMESE SLAW

PAPAYA | CUCUMBER | CILANTRO

Colorful and zesty. This slaw is perfect as a refreshing side dish with a number of warm foods or as a perfect filling in the Banh Mi Burger (page 119)! And it's done in a flash!

Juice of 1 lime
2 tablespoons (30 ml) soy sauce or tamari
3½ ounces (100 g) green papaya or daikon radish, julienned
3½ ounces (100 g) cucumber, thinly sliced
1¼ cups (20 g) fresh cilantro leaves, finely minced
1½ tablespoons (6 g) fresh mint leaves, finely minced
1 small red onion, thinly sliced
2 tablespoons plus 1 teaspoon (20 g) sesame seeds

In a large bowl, whisk the lime juice and soy sauce. Add the remaining ingredients and toss to combine. It's ready to serve.

Makes 10½ ounces (300 g)

HOISIN SAUCE

SOY | SESAME | RICE VINEGAR | COCONUT SUGAR

Chinese hoisin sauce is one of the world's most renowned sauces and is easy to make at home.

Adding a little sweetness to nutty sesame and savory soy sauce gives it a heavenly flavor. Hoisin sauce is excellent paired with hot Sriracha, and is not only a delicious veggie burger sauce, it's also perfect for stir-fries and a regular add-in to Asian soups. You might want to make extra batches to have handy.

3 tablespoons plus 1 teaspoon (50 ml) soy sauce or tamari
3 tablespoons (27 g) coconut sugar or (45 g) packed brown sugar
2 tablespoons (30 ml) sesame oil
2 tablespoons (30 ml) rice vinegar
2 tablespoons (30 g) tahini
2 cloves garlic, crushed
1 tablespoon (15 g) Sriracha
Pinch freshly ground black pepper

In a small saucepan over medium-high heat, combine all the ingredients. Bring to a boil, reduce the heat to low, and simmer the sauce for a few minutes until it thickens, stirring frequently. Let cool and use immediately or refrigerate, covered, for 1 to 2 weeks.

Makes about 3½ fluid ounces (100 ml)

Asian bbq Sauce
(page 102)

FORBIDDEN BURGER

BLACK RICE | BLACK BEANS | SHIITAKE | SPICY BROCCOLI | HOISIN SAUCE

This burger takes inspiration from the Orient, mixing black rice, black beans, savory shiitake, and hoisin sauce. You can make Hoisin Sauce at home (page 104) or buy a quality brand from a natural food store or your local grocery store. The highly nutritious black rice is also called "forbidden rice" because in ancient times it was only allowed to be eaten by the emperor of China.

1. To make the Spicy Broccoli: Heat up a pan to high heat and flash-fry the broccoli quickly in a dry pan for a minute. Sprinkle with red pepper flakes and a little salt, and drizzle with toasted sesame oil. Remove from the pan and keep covered until serving.

2. To make the patties: Place a skillet over medium-high heat and add a drizzle of vegetable oil. Fry the shiitake mushrooms for 8 to 10 minutes, or until golden and fragrant. Season to taste with salt and pepper. Remove from the heat and transfer to a large bowl.

3. Combine the mushrooms with the rest of the patty ingredients. Taste and add more salt or pepper if needed. Refrigerate the mixture for 30 minutes, or up to 24 hours covered.

4. Divide the mixture into 4 equal portions and shape each into a patty. Place a skillet over medium-high heat and add a drizzle of vegetable oil. Fry the patties for 2 to 4 minutes per side and serve immediately with a generous amount of Hoisin Sauce, Spicy Broccoli, bean sprouts, and mayo.

Makes 4 burgers

For Spicy Broccoli
7 ounces (200 g) steamed broccoli florets
½–1 teaspoon red pepper flakes
Salt
A drizzle of toasted sesame oil

For Patties
Vegetable oil, for frying
3½ ounces (100 g) shiitake mushrooms
1 cup (200 g) cooked black rice
1 can (14 ounces, or 400 g) black beans, drained, rinsed, and mashed with a fork
2 cloves garlic, crushed
2 scallions, thinly sliced
½ teaspoon fresh lemon juice
¾ teaspoon salt, plus more for seasoning
¼ teaspoon freshly ground black pepper, plus more for seasoning
3 tablespoons plus 1 teaspoon (52 g) Hoisin Sauce (page 104)
1 tablespoon nutritional yeast
1½ cups (75 g) panko or fine bread crumbs
1 tablespoon (15 ml) olive oil

4 bread buns (For black buns, see left.)

For Toppings
Hoisin Sauce (page 104)
Fresh bean sprouts
Mayonnaise (page 152)

PITCH-BLACK BUNS!
Create an extra-dramatic effect by serving your burgers in a black bun. They're so easy to make. Add 1 tablespoon (3 g) edible charcoal powder to your flour and the result will be deeply black burgers. Charcoal has a very subtle, almost unnoticeable, flavor. You'll find recipes for burger buns on pages 51 and 67.

KIMCHI

CABBAGE | GARLIC | GOCHUGARU | GINGER

Kimchi is Korean for pickle. On Western restaurant menus it usually means a delicious salt-and-chile pickled cabbage dish, but in fact you can "kimchi" a variety of vegetables. Traditionally, kimchi pickles sit for a few days to ferment, and that boosts the healthy bacteria culture and sour tang.

Kimchi can be spicy and it's traditionally made with Korean chili powder, gochugaru. You can use other chiles with delicious results. Kimchi needs to be stored in sterile airtight jars and used within 2 to 3 weeks (though it can last for several months). Kimchi is a powerful topping, adding interest not only to burgers but also to wok dishes, fried eggs, sandwiches, stews, and salads.

You need 1 or more large sterilized jars with lids. In a large bowl, mix together all the ingredients. Fill the jars, leaving just a little air space at the top. You can eat the kimchi straight away or seal the lid(s) and let it ferment for 2 to 3 days on the kitchen counter. Open the lid(s) and release any built-up gas pressure daily. Refrigerate the kimchi when the fermented taste reaches your preferred level.

Makes about 2¼ pounds (1 kg)

About 2¼ pounds (1 kg) chopped mixed cabbage and vegetables

About 5 tablespoons (2½ ounces, or 75 g) fine sea salt

4 cloves garlic, crushed

2 to 4 tablespoons (30 to 60 g) gochugaru or Sriracha, or other chili sauce of choice

2 tablespoons (30 ml) soy sauce or tamari

1½ tablespoons (9 g) grated fresh ginger

Hot Stuff!

FLAVOR VARIATIONS

Add one or more of these ingredients for a twist: seaweed, nuts and seeds, spring onions, or fruit, such as mango or berries.

KIMCHI MEE

KIMCHI | CILANTRO PISTOU | BLACK PEPPER TOFU

This is a Korean-inspired veggie burger and a variation of the Banh Mi Burger on page 119. I just love adding kimchi to my breads, and it pairs perfectly with the sweet-and-peppery seared tofu. I've also added micro sprouts for an extra fresh and nourishing crunch. A dollop of mayonnaise and a generous spoonful of Cilantro Pistou makes this burger a wonderful blend of spicy and fresh flavors.

1. To make the tofu: Place the tofu block on a plate lined with paper towels, and place another plate on top of the tofu. Gently press out any excess liquid by squeezing the plates together, being careful not to break up the tofu.

2. Slice the tofu into 4 flat pieces. Place a skillet over medium-low heat. Sear the tofu in the skillet for about 8 minutes per side. Top with the Kimchi, Cilantro Pistou, cucumbers and carrots, micro sprouts, and mayo. Squeeze a lime wedge over each burger and serve.

Makes 4 burgers

For Tofu

1 block (14 ounces, or 400 g) firm tofu, sliced crosswise into ¼-inch (6 mm) thick slices, cut to fit the breads

Drizzle of agave syrup or honey

Salt and freshly ground black pepper, to taste

4 breads, such as small rustic pieces of Ciabatta or baguette, halved and lightly toasted

For Toppings

Kimchi (page 110)

Cilantro Pistou (page 73)

Fresh cucumber and carrot sticks

Micro sprouts (optional)

Mayonnaise (page 152)

Lime wedges

SUSHI MINI BURGER

RICE BUNS | AVOCADO | GARI | NORI | WASABI MAYO

Sushi burgers are popular eye candy on social media—and turning sushi into mini burgers will be a popular party trick! It's incredibly easy to make the rice buns using cookie molds stuffed with cooked rice, a fun way to use leftover rice. This burger is layered with fresh flavors along with a hit of pungent wasabi and pretty gari (also known as pickled ginger)—it's guaranteed to be an interesting bite!

1. To make the rice buns: Fill 8 round mini cookie molds (about 1 inch [30 mm] in diameter) with the rice. Pat the tops flat. Cover with plastic wrap and refrigerate for 1 hour, or up to a few hours.

2. To make the Soy and Black Pepper Tofu: In a wide shallow bowl, stir together the soy sauce and honey. Place the tofu block on a plate lined with paper towels, and place another plate over the tofu. Gently press out any excess liquid by squeezing the plates together, being careful not to break up the tofu. Transfer the tofu to a cutting board and slice crosswise into ¼-inch (6 mm) thick pieces, and then into squares that will be your "patties."

3. Place a skillet over medium-high heat and add a drizzle of vegetable oil. Add the tofu pieces, season with the pepper, and fry for 3 to 5 minutes per side until golden. Transfer the tofu to the sweetened soy sauce and carefully turn to coat both sides. Place the pieces back in the skillet and fry for 1 minute more on each side.

4. Assemble the burgers: Placing a nori ribbon under the bottom of each rice bun, layer Wasabi Mayo, tofu, and toppings between the rice buns. Wrap the mini burger on the top rice bun, sealing the nori ribbon by wetting and pressing the ribbon ends together gently. Sprinkle with the sesame seeds and serve with soy sauce and sushi vinegar.

Makes 8 mini burgers

For Rice Buns

4 cups (744 g) cooked brown or sushi rice (1 cup rice per burger)

Black sesame seeds, for sprinkling

For Soy and Black Pepper Tofu

2 tablespoons (30 ml) soy sauce or tamari

½ teaspoon honey or agave syrup

1 block (7 ounces, or 200 g) extra firm tofu

Vegetable oil, for frying

1 teaspoon freshly ground black pepper

For Toppings and Dips

Wasabi Mayo (page 127)

Very thinly sliced gari (Pickled Ginger, page 117)

Avocado slices (rounds)

Thinly sliced radish (use watermelon radishes if you can find them)

½ cucumber, cut into thin sticks

1 sheet nori, cut into 8 ribbons

Soy sauce or tamari, for dipping

Sweet sushi vinegar, for dipping

SEA VEGETABLES!

Seaweed offers a variety of complex flavors, from powerful saline to subtle herbal notes. It's especially good for creating a seafood flavor in veggie burgers. Use seaweed in patties and as toppings for your burgers. Top left: Hijiki; top right: nori; bottom left: dulse; bottom right: wakame salad.

PICKLED GINGER

GINGER | RICE VINEGAR | AGAVE SYRUP

The delicious pinkish pickled ginger used for sushi is commonly known as gari in Japan. The pretty pink color comes from the pink tips on fresh young ginger roots. You can pickle older ginger too but serious sushi lovers prefer the young ginger.

3½ ounces (100 g) young ginger, peeled and thinly sliced
1 teaspoon salt, divided
6 tablespoons plus 2 teaspoons (100 ml) rice vinegar
2 tablespoons (40 g) agave syrup or honey

1. Place the ginger slices in a small bowl, sprinkle with ½ teaspoon salt, and let sit for 5 minutes.

2. Bring a small saucepan filled with water to a boil over high heat, add the ginger, reduce the heat to low, and simmer the ginger for 2 minutes. Drain the ginger well and place on a clean kitchen towel to absorb any excess water. Place the ginger in a half-pint (280 ml) Mason jar.

3. In a small saucepan over medium-high heat, combine the vinegar, agave syrup, and remaining ½ teaspoon salt. Cook until the vinegar's scent softens, about 2 minutes. Remove from the heat, let cool, and pour the mixture into the Mason jar with the ginger. Seal the jar and let it pickle in the refrigerator for a minimum of 4 hours.

Makes about 3½ ounces (100 g)

BANH MI BURGER

TOFU | SRIRACHA MAYO | VIETNAMESE SLAW

This burger is a perfect marriage of East and West flavors. During the French colonial days in Vietnam, the French brought their signature bread—the baguette—to Vietnam with them. Little did they know this would create fusion food history, as the Banh Mi was born: delicious French bread filled with Vietnamese flavors such as lime, cilantro, and savory tofu! Utterly delicious.

1. To make the marinade: In a small bowl, whisk the marinade ingredients until smooth. Transfer to a shallow baking dish.

2. To make the patties: Place the tofu block on a plate lined with paper towels, and place another plate on top of the tofu. Gently press out any excess liquid by squeezing the plates together, being careful not to break up the tofu. Slice the tofu into 4 flat pieces and put them into the marinade. Let sit for 30 minutes.

3. Place a skillet over medium-low heat. Remove the tofu from the marinade and sear it in the skillet for about 8 minutes per side. Serve on the baguette with the slaw, avocado, and mayo. Squeeze a bit of lime juice over each one.

Makes 4 burgers

For Marinade

2 tablespoons (30 ml) soy sauce or tamari

2 tablespoons (30 ml) mirin

2 tablespoons (31 g) Hoisin Sauce (page 104) or store-bought

1 tablespoon (15 ml) rapeseed oil

1 tablespoon (9 g) coconut sugar or (15 g) packed brown sugar

1 clove garlic, crushed

½ teaspoon grated fresh ginger

For Patties

1 block (10½ ounces, or 300 g) firm tofu, drained

1 baguette, sliced into 4 burger-sized portions

For Toppings

Vietnamese Slaw (page 104)

Avocado slices

Sriracha Mayo (page 128)

Lime wedges

SEITAN BURGER

SATAY SAUCE | SPICY SEITAN | BEAN SPROUTS

Inspired by Indonesian flavors, this dish is a delight for peanut lovers. Creamy peanut sauce, a.k.a. satay sauce, spiked with coconut and tamarind is the perfect companion to bean sprouts and spicy seitan. Seitan is a by-product of yeast. Here it's used like an Asian version of faux pulled pork rather than formed into a firmer patty. It's scrumptious with savory sauces like satay or other curries. You'll find seitan in Asian supermarkets or natural foods stores. You can easily substitute seitan with other ingredients such as tofu, tempeh, roasted vegetables, or beans.

For Spicy Seitan
¼ cup (60 ml) soy sauce or tamari
2 tablespoons (30 g) Sriracha
14 ounces (400 g) seitan in brine, drained
Vegetable oil, for frying
1 cup plus 2 teaspoons (250 ml) Satay Sauce (see right)

4 buns, halved and lightly toasted

For Toppings
Fresh cilantro leaves
Cucumber slices
Fresh bean sprouts
Roughly crushed peanuts
Finely sliced scallions or red onion

1. In a shallow dish, mix the soy sauce and Sriracha. Toss with the seitan in a bowl, making sure the seitan is well coated with the Sriracha mixture.

2. Place a skillet over medium-high heat and add a drizzle of vegetable oil. Fry the seitan slices for 4 to 5 minutes per side until golden.

3. Add the Satay Sauce and fry together for 2 minutes.

4. Assemble the burgers with the sauce between the warm buns and layer with cilantro, cucumber, bean sprouts, peanuts, and scallions.

Makes 4 burgers

SATAY SAUCE

PEANUTS | TAMARIND | COCONUT

Satay sauce is possibly one of the most delicious sauces ever invented! And despite having a reputation as indulgent, peanuts contain plenty of essential goodness such as folate, manganese, amino acids, and vitamin E. Lime, tamarind, ginger, garlic, and coconut give this creamy sauce an edge that elevates the peanuts into a heavenly sauce for burgers and skewers. Satay sauce originates from Southeast Asia where tamarind is used frequently in cooking. It adds a sweet-and-sour flavor that's essential in many Southeast Asian dishes. If you can't find tamarind paste, use Worcestershire sauce or ketchup instead, which both contain tamarind.

3½ ounces (100 g) raw peanuts
¾ teaspoon salt
Vegetable oil, for frying
2 banana shallots, finely sliced
¾ cup plus 1 tablespoon plus 2 teaspoons (200 ml) coconut milk or cream of choice
1¾ ounces (50 g) desiccated coconut
3 tablespoons (45 ml) soy sauce or tamari
2 tablespoons (18 g) coconut sugar
2 cloves garlic, crushed
Juice of 1 lime
1 tablespoon (14 g) tamarind paste
Pinch cayenne pepper

1. Preheat the oven to 400°F (200°C). Spread the peanuts on a rimmed baking sheet and roast for 5 minutes, shaking and tossing the nuts after 3 minutes. Transfer to a food processor, add the salt, and process the peanuts into a smooth butter.

2. Place a skillet over medium-high heat and add a drizzle of vegetable oil. Add the shallots and fry until translucent. Stir in the remaining ingredients and the peanuts and let the sauce simmer for 3 to 4 minutes. Remove from the heat. Refrigerate in an airtight container for 3 to 4 days.

Makes about 1 cup (250 ml)

TIP!
You can skip the peanut roasting step by using 3½ ounces (about 6 heaping tablespoons, or 100 g) peanut butter instead of whole peanuts.

Curried burgers

BOMBAY BURGER

CAULIFLOWER | TURMERIC | LIME CASHEW CREAM | SESAME-CARROT SALAD

Curry spices are both comforting and invigorating, and when mixed with cauliflower they make a powerful flavor experience! This patty gets its beautiful golden color from turmeric, the little root that's been making headlines as a superfood. Turmeric has a healing effect on our bodies when it's eaten regularly—something the rich cooking tradition of India has made good use of for thousands of years is now acknowledged by studies in the West. This delicious curry patty is accompanied by a sesame-carrot salad and lime cashew cream for vegan goodness!

1. Preheat the oven to 350°F (180°C).

2. To make the Lime Cashew Cream: In a blender or food processor, combine all the ingredients for the cashew cream and process until smooth. Set aside.

3. To make the Sesame-Carrot Salad: In a medium-sized bowl, stir together the carrot ribbons, vinegar, and sesame oil until well coated. Set aside.

4. To make the patties: Place a skillet over medium-high heat and add 1 tablespoon (15 ml) oil or (14 g) ghee. Add the onion and fry for 4 to 5 minutes, or until translucent. Transfer to a large bowl. Add another tablespoon (15 ml) oil or (14 g) ghee and the cauliflower, garlic, turmeric, garam masala, ginger, salt, and red pepper flakes. Fry for 6 to 8 minutes, stirring. Transfer to the bowl with the onion.

   Add the remaining patty ingredients to the bowl and mix to combine. Working in batches, pulse the mixture in a food processor for a few spins until the rice and oats are broken up. Be careful not to over blend—you want a crumbly texture. Refrigerate the mixture for 30 minutes, or up to 24 hours covered.

5. Divide the mixture into 4 equal portions and shape each into a patty. Place a skillet over medium-high heat and add the remaining tablespoon (15 ml) of oil or tablespoon (14 g) ghee. Fry the patties for 4 to 8 minutes per side. Lightly season with salt and pepper and transfer them to a rimmed baking sheet and bake for 8 to 10 minutes.

6. Assemble the burgers between the warm buns and serve topped with the Lime Cashew Cream and Sesame-Carrot Salad.

Makes 4 burgers, 8½ ounces (240 g) Lime Cashew Cream, and 10½ ounces (300 g) Sesame-Carrot Salad

For Lime Cashew Cream

1½ cups (200 g) cashews soaked for 1 to 3 hours in enough water to cover and drained

Juice of 1 lime

1 teaspoon honey or agave syrup

Pinch salt

Water, to thin

For Sesame-Carrot Salad

5 rainbow or regular carrots, peeled and shaved into ribbons

3 tablespoons (45 ml) rice vinegar

1 tablespoon (15 ml) toasted sesame oil

For Patties

3 tablespoons (45 ml) vegetable oil or (42 g) ghee, divided

½ cup (80 g) finely diced onion

2 cups (220 g) cauliflower, grated

3 cloves garlic, crushed

1 tablespoon (6 g) grated fresh turmeric

1 tablespoon (6 g) garam masala

1 teaspoon grated fresh ginger

¾ teaspoon salt, plus more to taste

½ teaspoon red pepper flakes

⅔ cup (100 g) rolled oats

½ cup (100 g) cooked brown rice

½ cup (75 g) toasted almonds, ground

½ cup (8 g) fresh cilantro leaves, finely minced

2 tablespoons plus 1 teaspoon (35 ml) fresh lemon juice

2 tablespoons (30 ml) rapeseed oil

1 tablespoon (4 g) nutritional yeast or grated Parmesan cheese

1 teaspoon coconut sugar

¼ teaspoon freshly ground black pepper

4 buns, halved and lightly toasted

THE LOYAL LENTIL BURGER

LENTILS | CUMIN | TURMERIC | CILANTRO | PICKLES | YOGURT

One of the most popular recipes I have created so far is a lentil curry that I call the Loyal Lentil Curry. In this recipe I adopted the curry's flavor for a lentil burger. And it's delicious. Cumin, cinnamon, and coriander make a delicious burger, smothered with a sweet yogurt sauce and topped with fresh cilantro and pickles. Add a few drops of lime juice as a finish.

1. To make the Yogurt Sauce: Mix the ingredients together in a bowl, cover, and refrigerate until assembly.

2. To make the patties: Place a skillet over medium-high heat and add a drizzle of vegetable oil. Fry the onion, garlic, and bell peppers for 5 to 7 minutes, or until the onion is transparent and golden.

3. Combine with the rest of the patty ingredients in a bowl, and adjust with more panko bread crumbs if the mixture feels too loose. Taste and adjust the seasoning.

4. Refrigerate the mixture for 30 minutes, or up to 24 hours covered.

5. Divide the mixture into 4 equal portions and shape each into a patty.

6. Place a skillet over medium-high heat and add a drizzle of vegetable oil. Fry the patties for 2 to 4 minutes per side, or until nicely browned.

7. Assemble the burgers and top each patty with Yogurt Sauce, pickles, and cilantro. Squeeze a lime wedge over each burger and serve.

Makes 4 burgers

For Yogurt Sauce

6¾ fluid ounces (200 ml) thick Greek yogurt or vegan yogurt
1 teaspoon agave syrup or honey
1 teaspoon fresh lime juice

For Patties

Vegetable oil, for frying
1 onion, finely sliced
3 cloves garlic, crushed
⅔ cup (100 g) diced red or green bell pepper
¾ cup (150 g) cooked dark lentils
1 scant cup (200 g) borlotti beans or black beans, drained, rinsed, and mashed with a fork
Zest and juice of 1 lime
1 teaspoon Sriracha or sambal sauce
1 tablespoon (15 ml) soy sauce
1 tablespoon (15 g) tahini
1 tablespoon (4 g) nutritional yeast or grated Parmesan cheese
½ teaspoon salt, plus more to taste
2 cups (100 g) panko bread crumbs or brown rice, plus more as needed
1½ teaspoon honey
1 teaspoon ground coriander
1½ teaspoons ground cumin
1 teaspoon ground or freshly grated turmeric
1 teaspoon ground cinnamon

4 buns, halved and lightly toasted

For Toppings

Yogurt Sauce
Pickles
Fresh cilantro
Lime wedges

TEMPEH BURGER

TEMPEH | CARROT MISO CREAM | DULSE | WASABI MAYO

Inspired by seaweed and South Asian flavors, this burger combines the fresh and invigorating flavors of Japanese wasabi, umeboshi, and ginger with savory miso and chunky-textured Indonesian tempeh. Top with Sweet Potato Crisps and slices of butter-soft avocado for a beautiful, textured bite!

For an extra aquatic flavor, I add "bacon of the sea" dulse. You will love the taste of this seaweed as it's packed full of deep umami satisfaction.

To make this burger, you don't need to combine the ingredients in a mixture or make a patty. Just slice, marinate, and fry the tempeh. Tempeh is made with fermented soybeans and has a lovely texture and firm bite, so it's a great meat replacement. Find tempeh, miso, rice vinegar, umeboshi, wasabi, and dulse in health foods stores, well-stocked grocery stores, or Asian markets.

1. Preheat the oven to 355°F (180°C).

2. To make the Wasabi Mayo: In a small bowl, whisk the mayonnaise and wasabi paste until smooth. Refrigerate until serving.

3. To make the Carrot Miso Cream: In a medium-sized bowl, mix together all the ingredients. Cover and keep refrigerated for 3 to 4 days.

4. To make the marinade: In a medium-sized bowl, whisk all the marinade ingredients and set aside.

5. To make the patties: Cut the tempeh in 4 (½-inch [1 cm]) slices. Lay them in a shallow bowl and pour the marinade over, making sure the tempeh is well coated. Let marinate for at least 20 minutes and up to 24 hours, covered, in the refrigerator.

   Remove the tempeh slices from the marinade. Place a skillet over medium-high heat and fry the tempeh for about 3 minutes per side until golden.

6. To assemble the burger: Start with a layer of Wasabi Mayo on the base bun followed by greens. Lay the tempeh on top, followed by the Carrot Miso Cream. After ensuring the excess moisture has been removed from the dulse, add it and top with avocado slices and Sweet Potato Crisps. Serve immediately.

Makes 4 burgers, about 1 cup (225 g) Wasabi Mayonnaise, and 7 ounces (200 g) Carrot Miso Cream

For Wasabi Mayo
1 scant cup (200 g) mayonnaise or vegan mayonnaise
2 teaspoons wasabi paste

For Carrot Miso Cream
5 medium carrots, peeled and grated
1½ tablespoons (24 g) yellow miso paste diluted in 1½ tablespoons (23 ml) warm water
1 tablespoon (15 ml) rice vinegar
1 tablespoon (15 ml) rapeseed oil
1 tablespoon (6 g) grated fresh ginger

For Marinade
3 tablespoons (45 ml) sesame oil
2 tablespoons (15 g) shichimi togarashi
2 tablespoons (40 ml) honey or agave syrup
2 tablespoons (30 ml) rice vinegar
1 tablespoon (16 g) umeboshi paste
1 tablespoon (15 ml) soy sauce or tamari
1 clove garlic, crushed

For Patties
14 ounces (400 g) tempeh

4 buns, halved and lightly toasted

For Toppings
Fresh greens
Handful of presoaked dulse, rinsed and washed
Sliced avocado
Sweet Potato Crisps (see Tip!)

TIP!
To make the Sweet Potato Crisps: Preheat the oven to 450°F (230°C). Peel and thinly sliced 1 sweet potato. Place the sweet potato slices on a rimmed baking sheet and bake for 15 minutes, or until crisp, turning halfway through the cooking time. Remove from the oven and let cool.

BALI BEACH BURGER

MUSHROOMS | WHITE BEANS | COCONUT | LEMONGRASS

This dreamy coconut and lemongrass veggie burger is inspired by Southeast Asian dishes that often combine sweet fruit and coconut with tangy lime and curry spices to create sensational flavor. Adding Mango Salsa or slices of fruit such as juicy watermelon is delicious, but they can be easily substituted with avocado and a few drops of lime juice.

1. To make the Mango Salsa: In a bowl, combine the salsa ingredients. Set aside.

2. To make the Sriracha Mayo: In a small bowl, combine the Sriracha and mayonnaise until well mixed. Refrigerate until ready to use.

3. To make the patties: Place a frying pan over medium-high heat and add a drizzle of vegetable oil. Add the mushrooms and fry for 5 to 7 minutes until shriveled and golden. Remove from the heat and transfer to a large bowl.

4. Add the remaining patty ingredients through the bread crumbs. Use your hands to work the mixture into a good texture that holds together. Season to taste with salt and pepper. Refrigerate the mixture for 30 minutes, or up to 24 hours covered.

5. Divide the mixture into 4 equal portions and shape each one into a patty.

6. Place a skillet over medium-high heat and add 1 tablespoon (14 g) coconut oil. Fry the patties for 2 to 4 minutes per side, or until nicely browned.

7. Assemble the burgers between the buns and spread with Sriracha Mayo and layer with fresh cilantro leaves and Mango Salsa. Add a few drops of toasted sesame oil and serve with lime wedges.

Makes 4 burgers, about 5 tablespoons Sriracha Mayo, and 1 cup (250 g) Mango Salsa

TIP!
Add extra crunch to this burger by sprinkling it with toasted crumbles of peanuts or cashew nuts, or topping with Root Crisps (page 138) or cripsy shallots. You can also exhange the Mango Salsa for the Cilantro Pistou on page 73.

For Mango Salsa
1 cup plus 2 tablespoons (200 g) diced fresh mango
Handful fresh cilantro leaves
Zest and juice of 1 lime

For Sriracha Mayo
1½ tablespoons Sriracha
¼ cup (56 g) mayonnaise (page 152)

For Patties
Vegetable oil, for frying
9 ounces (250 g) shiitake mushrooms, roughly chopped
¼ cup (50 g) cooked brown rice
1 cup (250 g) drained and rinsed canned white beans, mashed with a fork
3 cloves garlic, crushed
3 tablespoons (45 ml) soy sauce or tamari
1 teaspoon freshly grated lemongrass, or minced store-bought
2 tablespoons (8 g) nutritional yeast
2 cups (100 g) panko or gluten-free bread crumbs
⅔ cup (50 g) shredded coconut
Salt and freshly ground black pepper, to taste
1 tablespoon (14 g) coconut oil

4 buns, halved and lightly toasted

For Toppings
Chopped scallion
Fresh cilantro leaves
Toasted sesame oil
Lime wedges

THE UNITED STATES & LATIN AMERICA

The Americas are synonymous with fantastic street food. Just think of Latin American tacos and tortillas or the scrumptious bagels and epic burgers of the United States.

America is the birthplace of the hamburger! The forefather of the veggie burger, of course. This chapter pays tribute to classic American flavors, but ditches the processed ingredients in favor of whole foods.

America has a rich mix of cultural heritages, with many world kitchens enriching American cuisine's kaleidoscope of flavors. Produce often associated with America is corn, squash, wheat, maple syrup, and pumpkin. In Latin America (and California), peppers, sweet potato, beans, and citrus fruits are popular in cooking. One of the healthier foods comes from Peru: Quinoa, with its exceptional health benefits, has become a world sensation and a frequent ingredient in veggie burgers.

This chapter is all about keeping what works and chucking the rest, serving up the next generation of burgers!

MUSHROOM FAJITAS

PORTOBELLO MUSHROOM | BELL PEPPERS | AVOCADO LIME CREAM

Fajitas are a Mexican beef dish that can be made vegetarian using seared portobello mushroom slices instead of beef. Fried peppers and a sour-and-savory spice marinade are typical. For an extra-smoky taste, add a teaspoon of liquid smoke. The fried vegetables should be served smoking hot! It's delicious accompanied by cool and refreshing cilantro and Avocado Lime Cream.

1. To make the Avocado Lime Cream: In a small bowl, mix together the avocado, cashew fraîche, and lime juice until smooth. Cover and refrigerate until assembly.

2. To make the sauce: In another small bowl, whisk the sauce ingredients and set aside.

3. To make the Fajita Veggies: Place a skillet over medium-high heat and add a drizzle of vegetable oil. Add the onion and fry for 5 minutes. Add the red, green, and yellow bell peppers. Fry for 15 minutes more, stirring. Remove from the heat and set aside, covered.

   Heat another skillet over medium-high heat and add a drizzle of vegetable oil. Fry the portobello slices until golden and shriveled. Season to taste with salt and pepper. Remove from the pan and keep covered.

   Return the skillet to the heat, increase the heat to high, and return the onion and peppers to the skillet. Splash with the sauce and stir-fry for 2 minutes. Season to taste with salt and pepper. Stir in the cilantro and remove from the heat.

4. Assemble the mushroom slices between warm buns and add cheese if you wish. Serve with Avocado Lime Cream.

Makes 4 burgers and about 5⅓ to 7 ounces (150 to 200 g) Avocado Lime Cream, depending on the size of your avocado

TIP!
Add a few Pimientos de Padrón to the fajita veggies for a fun twist. Some of the padron peppers are hot and others not, so it can add a surprise element to the meal. Not a hot tip for eaters with faint taste buds or for small children.

For Avocado Lime Cream
1 avocado, halved, pitted, and peeled
1¾ ounces (50 g) cashew fraîche or crème fraîche
1 tablespoon (15 ml) fresh lime juice

For Sauce
6 tablespoons plus 2 teaspoons (100 ml) fresh lime juice
2 tablespoons (30 ml) olive oil
2 cloves garlic, crushed
1 teaspoon freshly ground black pepper
½ teaspoon chipotle powder
¼ teaspoon ground cumin
1 teaspoon liquid smoke (optional)

For Fajita Veggies
Vegetable oil, for frying
2 red onions, sliced into thin strips
1 red bell pepper, sliced into thin strips
1 green bell pepper, sliced into thin strips
1 yellow bell pepper, sliced into thin strips
4 portobello mushrooms, stemmed and sliced
1 cup (16 g) fresh cilantro leaves, chopped
Salt and freshly ground black pepper, to taste

4 buns, halved and lightly toasted
4 slices cheese or vegan cheese

Your majesty!

THE TRUFFLED BURGER QUEEN

LENTILS | CASHEWS | TRUFFLE MAYONNAISE | SWEET POTATO

This delicious lentil and black bean burger comes with a little extra of everything. It's stuffed with roasted nuts, Parmesan cheese, hot chili sauce, and sweetness from balsamic vinegar. I made this recipe for a relative who loves hamburgers and he loved this veggie burger so much he asked for the recipe! Truffle mayonnaise adds an extra layer of deliciousness to this royal veggie burger.

1. To make the patties: Place a skillet over medium-high heat and add 1 tablespoon (15 ml) of olive oil or (14 g) of ghee for frying. Add the onions and fry until transparent and fragrant, add the green bell pepper and garlic during the last minute of frying. Transfer to a large bowl and combine with the remaining patty ingredients through the pepper.

2. Refrigerate the mixture for 30 minutes, or up to 24 hours covered.

3. Divide the mixture into 4 equal portions and shape each into a patty. Place a skillet over medium-high heat and add a drizzle of olive oil or 1 tablespoon (14 g) ghee. Fry the patties for 2 to 5 minutes per side, or until nicely browned.

4. To make the Truffle Mayo: Mix the ingredients together into a smooth sauce.

5. Assemble the burgers on the toasted buns with the toppings.

Makes 4 burgers

For Patties
Olive oil or ghee, for frying
1 yellow onion, finely sliced
1 green bell pepper, diced small
2 cloves garlic, crushed
¾ cup (100 g) roasted cashews, chopped
½ cup (100 g) cooked and drained green lentils
½ cup plus 3 tablespoons (150 g) drained and rinsed canned black beans, mashed with a fork
1 cup (100 g) grated Parmesan cheese or Rawmesan (page 58)
2 cups (100 g) panko or gluten-free bread crumbs
1 tablespoon (15 g) chili sauce
1 teaspoon balsamic vinegar
¾ teaspoon salt, plus more to taste
¼ teaspoon pepper
1 teaspoon agave syrup

4 buns, halved and lightly toasted

For Truffle Mayo
1 scant cup (200 g) mayonnaise or vegan mayonnaise (page 152)
1 tablespoon (15 ml) truffle oil, or more to taste
Salt and freshly ground black pepper, to taste
A few drops of fresh lemon juice

For Toppings
Sweet potato slices
Pickled Onion (page 30)
Fresh green leaves or herbs
Fresh cherry tomatoes

GRILL BURGER

BLACK BEANS | CARAMELIZED ONIONS | BBQ SAUCE

This recipe is a great all-around recipe for a grilled veggie burger. Black beans and rice give a firmer hold and you can tweak it with a variety of spices. Explore the variety of interesting chiles—this burger favors the ancho! Ancho is the dried version of a poblano pepper hailing from Mexico. It is rather mild in its heat level and adds just enough spiciness to make it interesting. Slather with a sweet-and-smoky Orange BBQ Sauce, caramelized onions, and, if you are feeling indulgent, a slice of mature hard cheese.

1. To make the patties: Preheat the oven to 425°F (220°C). Line a rimmed baking sheet with parchment paper. Spread the black beans, garlic, and mushrooms on the prepared sheet. Drizzle with oil and sprinkle with salt. Roast for 20 minutes, turning everything over halfway through the cooking time. Remove from the oven. Mash the garlic with a fork and chop the roasted mushrooms small. Transfer to a large bowl and add the remaining patty ingredients.

2. In a food processor, pulse the mixture in batches until the texture is rough, crumbly, and sticky. Taste and adjust the seasonings with more salt and pepper if needed. Refrigerate the mixture for 15 to 30 minutes, or up to 24 hours covered. If you need to start an outdoor grill, now is the time to preheat it to medium-high heat.

3. Divide the mixture into 4 equal portions and shape each into a patty. Season to taste with salt and pepper. Place the patties on the grill and grill for about 2 minutes per side until you see desirable char marks, or they are nicely browned, or longer if you like a more grilled taste and look. Alternatively, you can cook the patties in a skillet or grill pan over medium-high heat, or cook for 15 to 20 minutes in a 400°F (200°C) oven.

4. Remove the burgers and assemble on the buns with the toppings and sauce.

Makes 4 burgers

For Patties

1⅓ cups (298 g) drained and rinsed canned black beans, mashed with a fork

2 cloves garlic

7 ounces (200 g) mushrooms, sliced

2 tablespoons (30 ml) olive oil or vegetable oil

¾ teaspoon salt, plus more to taste

1¾ ounces (50 g) walnuts, ground

2 cups (100 g) panko or regular bread crumbs

¼ cup (50 g) cooked brown rice

2 tablespoons (8 g) nutritional yeast or grated Parmesan cheese

1 tablespoon (11 g) mustard

1 tablespoon (15 ml) balsamic vinegar

1 teaspoon ancho chile powder or other chile

1 teaspoon mild chili powder

¼ teaspoon freshly ground black pepper

4 buns, halved and lightly toasted on the grill

For Toppings

Orange BBQ Sauce (page 138)
4 slices cheese or vegan cheese
Caramelized Onions (page 32)

ORANGE BBQ SAUCE

ORANGE | FENNEL SEEDS | LIQUID SMOKE

A good BBQ sauce is indispensable when the grilling starts—the slightly sweet and tart components create a delicious balance to charred and savory food. This sauce can be used to add flavor to patties and as a sauce to top the burgers. Orange juice and zest add a lovely sweet interest to this sauce and liquid smoke adds a wonderful smoky flavor that enhances the food whether you are panfrying, oven roasting, or grilling it, but you can skip it and the sauce is still delicious. Find liquid smoke in specialty culinary stores or in vegan shops online. Make a big batch of this sauce and use for all your grilled dishes.

Vegetable oil or ghee, for frying
¼ cup plus 3 tablespoons (70 g) finely diced shallot or red onion
4 cloves garlic, crushed
6 tablespoons plus 2 teaspoons (100 ml) fresh orange juice
Zest of 1 orange
6 tablespoons plus 2 teaspoons (100 g) ketchup
⅓ cup (75 g) packed brown sugar or coconut sugar
3 tablespoons plus 1 teaspoon (50 ml) apple cider vinegar
2 tablespoons (30 ml) soy sauce or tamari
2 tablespoons (30 ml) liquid smoke (optional)
1 tablespoon (15 g) Dijon mustard
1 tablespoon (15 g) Sriracha or chili sauce of choice
1½ teaspoons *pimentón* (smoked paprika)
1½ teaspoons ground fennel seeds
½ teaspoon salt
¼ teaspoon freshly ground black pepper

Place a skillet over medium heat. Add a drizzle of vegetable oil or 1 teaspoon ghee. Add the shallot and garlic and fry for 10 minutes, or until the shallot is translucent. Stir in the remaining ingredients and let the sauce simmer for 20 minutes, stirring occasionally to avoid burning. Remove from the heat. If you like a smooth sauce, blend in a food processor to perfection. Refrigerate in an airtight container for up to 1 week.

Makes 17 fluid ounces (500 ml)

ROOT CRISPS

ROASTED ROOT VEGETABLE SLICES

Root vegetables add crunch and a savoriness as a burger topping. Have fun mixing root vegetables of different colors or stick to a favorite. You can also enjoy the crisps as snacks with a variety of cold sauces from this book such as the Dill and Mustard Cashew Sauce (page 152), Muhammara (page 92), or New Caesar Dressing (page 58).

About 1 lb (500 g) mixed root vegetables such as sweet potatoes, Stokes Purple sweet potatoes, beets, and potatoes, peeled and sliced thin (2-3 mm)
1 tablespoon (15 ml) olive oil
Salt and freshly ground pepper, to taste

1. Preheat the oven to 300°F (160°C).

2. Place the vegetable slices in a bowl. Drizzle or spray with olive oil, and sprinkle with salt and pepper.

3. Line two baking sheet with parchment paper and place the vegetable slices on them without overlapping. Roast for 20 minutes in the middle of the oven; watch carefully for the last 5 minutes to avoid burning. Flip the crisps and roast for another 10 to 15 minutes. Check the oven frequently to avoid burning.

Makes 10 servings

TIP!
Sprinkle the crisps with spices and herbs for extra flavor. Try nutritional yeast or *pimentón* (smoked paprika) for a stronger flavor, or try fragrant herbs such as thyme or rosemary.

Avocado adds a healthy fat taste to the veggie burgers, and it also enhances the other flavors such as hot chiles and earthy spices.

FUTURE CLASSIC VEGGIE BURGER

MUSHROOM | LENTILS | LIQUID SMOKE | ROOT CRISPS

This veggie burger is versatile and the flavors are meant to mimic the savory bites of meat burgers. The patty is a great starting point to build a classic burger with your favorite toppings—like mayo, ketchup, cheese, onion, tomatoes, lettuce, and more. Here, I mix up a classic ketchup and mayo mix and add fresh cherry tomatoes to top the burger, along with homemade root crisps for extra crunch. You can also use quality root crisps from a natural foods shop.

Lentils are one of my favorite main ingredients for veggie burgers. They don't hold the burger together as well as black beans but, when seasoned right, carry the flavor fantastically.

1. To make the Classic Sauce: In a small bowl, stir together the mayonnaise and ketchup until smooth. Refrigerate until assembly.

2. To make the patties: Place a skillet over medium-high heat and add 1 tablespoon (15 ml olive oil or 14 g ghee) fat for frying. Add the mushrooms and fry for 5 to 7 minutes, stirring, or until fragrant and shriveled in size. Transfer to a large bowl and combine with the remaining patty ingredients (through pepper). Refrigerate the mixture for 30 minutes, or up to 24 hours covered.

3. Divide the mixture into 4 equal portions and shape each into a patty. Place a skillet over medium-high heat and add a drizzle of olive oil or 1 tablespoon (14 g) ghee. Fry the patties for 4 to 6 minutes per side, or until nicely browned.

4. Assemble the burgers on the toasted buns with the toppings.

Makes 4 burgers and ¼ cup (60 g) Classic Sauce

For Classic Sauce
3 tablespoons (42 g) mayonnaise or vegan mayonnaise (page 152)
1 tablespoon (15 g) ketchup

For Patties
Olive oil or ghee, for frying
About 9 ounces (250 g) mushrooms
1 cup (200 g) cooked, rinsed, and drained black or dark green lentils
1 cup (100 g) back beans, cooked, drained, and mashed with a fork
1 tablespoon (3 g) fresh thyme leaves
1½ scant cups (70 g) panko or regular bread crumbs
6½ tablespoons (80 g) cooked brown rice
2 tablespoons (8 g) fresh parsley leaves, finely chopped
½ cup (50 g) grated Parmesan cheese or Rawmesan (page 58)
1½ tablespoons (23 g) Sriracha
2 tablespoons (30 ml) soy sauce or tamari
2 cloves garlic, crushed
1 tablespoon (4 g) rubbed thyme
1 tablespoon (15 ml) balsamic vinegar
1 tablespoon (15 ml) liquid smoke (optional)
1 teaspoon *pimentón* (smoked paprika)
¾ teaspoon salt, plus more to taste
¼ teaspoon freshly ground black pepper, plus more to taste

4 buns, halved and lightly toasted

For Toppings
4 slices cheese of choice (optional)
Root Crisps (see page 138)
Classic Sauce
Sliced cherry tomatoes

TIP!
Add 1 tablespoon (15 ml)
liquid smoke to the mixture
for an extra-smoky flavor.

SAGE AND SQUASH BURGER

SAGE | BUTTERNUT SQUASH | BLUE CHEESE | PEAR | LEMONY CASHEW CREAM

During pumpkin and squash season you might want to use the sweet creamy flesh of squashes in your veggie burgers! This roasted butternut squash and sage burger with crumbles of blue cheese is great for weekend lunches and gatherings. The butternut squash needs to roast but during this time you can prepare the rest of the ingredients, set the table, or have a cup of tea! There are different textures at play in this patty, with walnuts, pear, and the rice adding firmness to the soft squash. The rice is pulsed separately to break it up and release the starch for extra blinding power. Blue cheese pairs well with butternut squash but can be omitted for a vegan burger.

1. To make the Lemony Cashew Cream: In a small bowl, whisk the cashew butter, nut milk, lemon juice, and salt until smooth. Cover and refrigerate until needed.

2. To make the patties: Preheat the oven to 400°F (200°C). In a small bowl, mix the sage with the olive oil. Rub the sage oil on the butternut squash and place it in a baking dish. Add the shallots and garlic. Roast for 40 minutes, turning halfway through the cooking time. Check that the butternut squash is cooked through by piercing it with a metal skewer—if it slides through the flesh easily, it's done. Remove and reset the oven temperature to 140°F (60°C). When the squash cools, remove the peel. Chop the flesh into small pieces and place them in a large bowl.

3. Fry the shallots and garlic with the kale for a couple of minutes until softened and fragrant. Add it to the bowl. Pulse the barley in a food processor to break it up into a crumbly texture and transfer it to the bowl. Add the remaining patty ingredients. Combine the ingredients with your hands into a sticky mixture. Transfer about a fifth of the mixture to a food processor and pulse it to a finer mix. Return it to the bowl and combine. If the mixture feels too wet, adjust by adding small amounts of panko.

4. Taste and adjust the seasonings with more salt and pepper if needed. Refrigerate the mixture for 15 minutes, or up to 24 hours covered.

5. Divide the mixture into 4 equal portions and shape each into a patty. Place a skillet over medium-high heat and add a drizzle of vegetable oil or 1 tablespoon (14 g) of ghee. Fry the patties for about 2 to 4 minutes per side. Lightly season with salt and pepper.

6. Serve the patties on the toasted buns topped with Lemony Cashew Cream, crispy sage, and pear slices.

Makes 4 burgers and about 6 fluid ounces (175 ml) Lemony Cashew Cream

For Lemony Cashew Cream

3½ ounces (about 6 heaping tablespoons, or 100 g) cashew butter or almond butter
¼ cup (60 ml) nut milk
1 tablespoon (15 ml) fresh lemon juice
Pinch of salt

For Patties

1 tablespoon (4 g) rubbed sage
1 tablespoon (15 ml) olive oil
½ (about 250 g) butternut squash, seeds removed
2 shallots, halved
3 cloves garlic, crushed
1¼ cups (80 g) stemmed and finely chopped kale
Scant ½ cup (70 g) cooked barley or brown rice
Scant ⅓ cup (100 g) drained and rinsed canned white beans or other firm beans, mashed with a fork
2 cups (100 g) panko or bread crumbs
⅓ cup (40 g) crumbled blue cheese, such as Roquefort (optional) or use vegan cheese
2½ ounces (70 g) roasted and ground sunflower seeds or other roasted seeds or nuts
2 tablespoons (8 g) nutritional yeast or Parmesan cheese
½ teaspoon red pepper flakes
¾ teaspoon salt, plus more to taste
¼ teaspoon freshly ground black pepper, plus more to taste
Vegetable oil or ghee, for frying

4 buns, halved and lightly toasted

For Toppings

Lightly toasted fresh sage leaves
Lemony Cashew Cream or sour cream
Pear slices

TIP!
As an alternative to Lemony Cashew Cream, simply mix
1/2 cup plus 3 tablespoons plus 1 teaspoon (150 g) sour
cream with a pinch of salt in a small bowl, cover, and
refrigerate until serving.

PULLED JACKFRUIT SLIDERS

JACKFRUIT | MANGO | SEAWEED

The meat-free version of pulled pork is often made with fleshy jackfruit. This juicy dish is brimming with flavor from salty nori flakes and homemade BBQ sauce. Top with mango and refreshing cilantro for that extra-summery taste. Topping with seaweed gives a taste of the ocean with plenty of mineral and umami flavor to mimic seafood. You can use other seaweeds in place of the nori; just follow the instructions for preparation, and chop or tear finely. Swap the mango for buttery avocado slices or papaya as a variation. A little squeeze of lime juice before serving adds a delicious, tangy finish!

1. To make the Pulled Jackfruit: Chop the jackfruit in thin smallish chunks, keeping the core, as it will soften. Place a skillet over medium-high heat, and add a drizzle of vegetable oil. Add the onions and fry for 8 to 10 minutes until it starts to caramelize. Stir in the jackfruit and vegetable broth. Add the garlic and nutritional yeast. Simmer the mixture for 10 minutes, stirring occasionally to break up the jackfruit. Add a little water if needed.

2. Add 1 tablespoon (15 ml) vegetable oil, the BBQ sauce, and Sriracha, and fry, stirring, for 15 minutes more. Add vegetable broth if it dries out too much. When the jackfruit is softened and the liquid has reduced, drizzle with the olive oil. Taste and adjust the seasoning if needed.

3. Remove and assemble the sliders with the buns, nori flakes, mango, and cilantro.

Makes 10 to 12 sliders or 6 to 8 burgers

For Pulled Jackfruit

2 cans (14 ounces, or 400 g each) green jackfruit in water, rinsed and drained (you'll have 15.8 ounces, or 550 g, jackfruit)

Vegetable oil or ghee, for frying

1 yellow onion, finely sliced

17 fluid ounces (500 ml) vegetable broth, plus more as needed

4 tablespoons (16 g) nutritional yeast

3 cloves garlic crushed

14 ounces (400 ml) BBQ sauce of your choice (Orange BBQ Sauce, page 138; Asian BBQ Sauce, page 102)

1 tablespoon (15 g) Sriracha

Extra-virgin olive oil

Salt and freshly ground black pepper, to taste

10 slider buns, tortillas, or pita pockets, halved and lightly toasted

For Toppings

Nori sheets (tear into pieces to top the patties), or use soaked and drained dulse or wakame

Slices of mango

Fresh cilantro

WATERMELON POKE BURGER

WATERMELON | RICE VINEGAR | SOY SAUCE | AVOCADO | PICKLED WAKAME

This appetizer is so fresh and full of exciting flavor contrasts you'll want to make it again and again, especially on hot summer days. It's really easy to put together and makes a great starter or mingle dish for parties. Combining sweet watermelon with a savory poke-soy sauce creates an exciting taste. The marinated watermelon slices are highlighted with fresh cilantro, creamy avocado, and sweet-and-peppery tofu.

1. To make the Poke Sauce: In a small bowl, stir together the vinegar, soy sauce, sesame oil, and lime juice.

2. Cut the watermelon into ½-inch (1 cm) thick slices and remove the rind. Using a round cookie cutter about 2 inches (3.5 cm, in diameter), cut out 8 small watermelon rounds from the slices. Carefully place the watermelon in a sealable plastic bag and pour in the vinegar sauce mixture. Seal the bag and refrigerate to marinate for 30 minutes.

3. Using the same size cookie cutters, cut 4 rounds from the tofu slices. Heat up a frying pan to medium-high heat and add a drizzle of oil. Fry the rounds on both sides for a couple of minutes until golden. Season with salt and pepper to taste, and drizzle with a little soy sauce.

4. Layer the tofu, avocado, cilantro, pickled wakame, and scallions between the watermelon rounds. Sprinkle with black sesame seeds.

Makes 4 burgers

For Poke Sauce
6 tablespoons plus 2 teaspoons (100 ml) rice vinegar
¼ cup (60 ml) soy sauce or tamari
2 tablespoons (30 ml) toasted sesame oil
2 tablespoons (30 ml) fresh lime juice (about 1 lime)

½ watermelon

For Tofu
1 block (300 g) firm tofu, sliced crosswise in about ½-inch (1 cm) thick slices
Vegetable oil, for frying
Salt and freshly ground black pepper, to taste
2 tablespoons (28 ml) soy sauce or tamari sauce

For Toppings
2 large-sized avocados, cut in rounds
1 cup plus 2 tablespoons (20 g) fresh cilantro leaves, chopped
Pickled wakame
2 scallions, finely diced
Black sesame seeds, for sprinkling

You can also try...

VARIATIONS
An alternative to tofu in this burger is swapping it for French semisoft goat cheese (about ⅓ cup [50 g] per burger). You can also skip both the tofu and the goat cheese and just serve with avocado and top with pickled wakame.

BEET AND QUINOA BURGER

BEET | QUINOA | CHIA SEEDS | SPROUTS | JALAPEÑO CASHEW CREAM

A burger never felt so nourishing before! This veggie burger uses Latin American superfoods such as protein-rich quinoa, super-nutritious chia seeds, and liver-cleansing beets. Quinoa adds a wonderful and delicate texture, while the raw grated beet gives a deep juicy flavor. I soak the chia seeds to make a vegan egg substitute, which adds binding power to the patties. To make things even more exciting, serve with chipotle mayo for an invigorating, fresh taste. This burger has a "rare" bite. It's soft and fragile, so handle with care in the pan.

1. To make the Jalapeño Cashew Cream: In a small bowl, mix the Lemony Cashew Cream, chives, and jalapeño until smooth. Add salt to taste, and stir in the agave. Refrigerate until serving.

2. To make the patties: Preheat the oven to 210°F (100°C). Place the quinoa in a saucepan filled with water and boil over high heat for 15 minutes. Drain in a fine-mesh sieve and set aside without covering to dry out any excess moisture. Fluff the quinoa with a fork.

3. Place a skillet over medium-high heat and add a drizzle of vegetable oil. Add the onion, garlic, and mushrooms. Fry for 6 to 7 minutes, stirring, or until the mushrooms are golden and shriveled.

4. Stir in the white beans, nutritional yeast, paprika, and cumin. Fry for 2 to 3 minutes, stirring, or until any excess liquid from the beans evaporates. Transfer to a large bowl.

5. Add the olive oil, chia egg, cooked quinoa, beets, cilantro, lime zest, oats, and salt. Combine the ingredients and refrigerate the mixture for 30 minutes or longer, or up to 24 hours covered.

6. Divide the mixture into 4 equal portions and shape each into a patty. Place a skillet over medium-low heat and add a drizzle of vegetable oil or ghee. Fry the patties for 5 minutes per side.

7. Assemble the burgers on the buns and dig in.

Makes 4 burgers

For Jalapeño Cashew Cream
6 tablespoons (100 g) Lemony Cashew Cream (page 142), crème fraîche, yogurt, or vegan yogurt

2 tablespoons (6 g) chives, finely chopped

1 jalapeño, pitted and finely minced

Salt, to taste

1 teaspoon agave syrup or honey

For Patties
Slightly more than 2 ounces (60 g) uncooked quinoa, rinsed well (yields 5⅓ ounces, or 150 g, cooked quinoa)

Vegetable oil or ghee, for frying

1 onion, finely diced

2 cloves garlic, crushed

7 ounces (200 g) mushrooms, finely chopped

8 ounces (227 g) drained and rinsed canned white beans, mashed with a fork

2 tablespoons (8 g) nutritional yeast or grated Parmesan cheese

1 teaspoon *pimentón* (smoked paprika)

¾ teaspoon ground cumin

2 tablespoons (30 ml) olive oil

1 chia egg (page 14) or hen's egg

5½ ounces (150 g) grated raw beets

3 tablespoons (3 g) chopped fresh cilantro

Zest of 1 lime

2½ ounces (70 g) rolled oats

½ teaspoon salt, plus more to taste

4 buns, halved and lightly toasted, or 4 portobello mushrooms buns (2 mushrooms per bun, page 70)

For Toppings
Baked sweet potato slices or avocado slices

Sprouts (optional)

TIP!
For a stunning effect, serve the patty with a black charcoal or green spirulina bun (page 108). Or, for more superfood power, use the Super Good Quinoa Spelt Buns (page 51).

A super burger!

AFTER BEACH BURGER

CHICKPEAS | AVOCADO | ARTICHOKE CRÈME | KIMCHI

This burger is hot and cool at the same time. The flavors are inspired by what I would like to eat after a day at the beach—something that's hydrating and satisfyingly savory. The chickpeas, lentils, and carrots add juiciness to the chewy cashews and the earthy spices. Topping the patty with hot kimchi next to a cool Dill and Mustard Cashew Sauce (page 152), with the addition of smooth and cool avocado, makes this a perfect contrasting-taste experience.

1. Preheat the oven to 145°F (60°C).

2. Prepare the Artichoke Crème (page 152) and Dill and Mustard Cashew Sauce (page 152).

3. To make the patties: Pulse the burger ingredients for a few seconds with a hand-held mixer or in a food processor, or break up the ingredients with a fork. Add more ground oats if the mixture feels too wet and loose. Taste and adjust with salt and pepper. Refrigerate for 30 minutes or longer, or up to 24 hours covered.

4. Divide the mixture into 4 equal portions and shape each into a patty. Place a skillet over medium-low heat and add a drizzle of vegetable oil or ghee.

5. Fry the patties for 2 minutes on both sides until golden and fragrant. They should be nicely golden brown when they're done. Salt lightly. Transfer the fried burgers to an oven tray and keep warm in the oven until assembly.

6. Layer the burgers by adding the toppings, and serve straight away.

Makes 4 burgers

For Patties

½ cup (100 g) cooked dark lentils

8 ounces (227 g) drained and rinsed canned chickpeas, mashed with a fork

1 cup (120 g) toasted cashew nuts, roughly ground

1 cup (50 g) panko or toasted oats, ground

2 carrots, grated

1 tablespoon (7 g) broken flaxseeds (optional)

2 tablespoons (30 ml) soy sauce

½ tablespoon (10 ml) fresh lemon juice

1 tablespoon (3 g) oregano or marjoram

½ tablespoon (4 g) paprika powder

½ cup (20 g) fresh basil, roughly chopped

⅓ cup (40 g) onion, finely diced

2 cloves garlic, crushed

½ tablespoon (8 g) sambal or Sriracha

½ tablespoon (10 ml) olive oil

1 teaspoon fine salt

Pinch of freshly ground black pepper

4 bread buns, halved

For Toppings

Artichoke Crème (page 152)

Dill and Mustard Cashew Sauce (page 152)

Kimchi (page 110) or Pink Kraut (page 42)

Fresh cucumber, finely sliced

Avocado slices

Handful of baby spinach or arugula

Pickled or Just Raw Onion (page 30)

SILKY TOFU MAYONNAISE

This vegan mayonnaise is a great base sauce for topping veggie burgers. Use it plain or add an extra flavor such as a tablespoon of mustard, Sriracha, freshly grated garlic, truffle tapenade, or lemon zest for an extra twist.

½ lb (200 g) silky tofu
1 teaspoon agave syrup
1½ tablespoons (25 ml) white vinegar
1 tablespoon (11 g) mustard
½ teaspoon salt, plus more to taste

Mix the ingredients together into a smooth sauce. Cover and refrigerate. Keeps for 3 to 4 days in the fridge.

Makes about 1¼ cup (300 g)

ARTICHOKE CRÈME

Fans of artichoke might want to dip into this delicious topping sauce.

½ cup (150 g) artichoke hearts, marinated in vinegar and oil
¼ cup (64 g) cannellini beans
2 tablespoons (10 g) Parmesan cheese, grated fine (Or substitute nutritional yeast.)
2 tablespoons (30 ml) extra-virgin olive oil
1 clove garlic
Juice of ½ lemon
Water to thin out if needed
Salt and freshly ground black pepper, to taste

1. Mix the ingredients together into a smooth sauce.

2. Cover and refrigerate. Keeps for 3 to 4 days in the fridge.

Makes about ¾ cup (200 g)

MAYONNAISE

Making your own mayonnaise is a great alternative to the store-bought versions. Use an egg from a biodynamic farm for the best flavor.

1 egg yolk
1 tablespoon (15 ml) white wine vinegar
1 tablespoon (11 g) mustard
5 fluid ounces (150 ml) mild olive oil
Salt, to taste

1. Leave the eggs, vinegar, mustard, and olive oil out of the fridge for a little while before you prepare the recipe. Start when your ingredients are all at room temperature.

2. In a bowl, whip the egg and vinegar together with the mustard and a little salt.

3. Add the oil while whipping, starting with a few drops. Slowly add more, taste, and add more. Taste and adjust the flavor with salt and vinegar if needed.

Makes about ¾ cup (175 g)

DILL AND MUSTARD CASHEW SAUCE

This deliciously cooling sauce is good with variety of flavors.

1 tablespoon (4 g) fresh dill, chopped fine
2 teaspoons honey
1 tablespoon (15 ml) almond milk
1 tablespoon (16 g) cashew butter
2 teaspoons Japanese rice vinegar for sushi (can be subbed for white wine vinegar)
1 teaspoon mild mustard
1 tablespoon (15 ml) olive oil
1 tablespoon (15 ml) fresh lemon juice
½ teaspoon fine salt

1. Mix the ingredients together into a smooth sauce.

2. Cover and refrigerate. Keeps for 3 to 4 days in the fridge.

Makes about ½ cup (90 g)

The Grill Burger (page 136) with
Root Crisps (page 138) and avocado

Veggie burger cheat sheet

INGREDIENTS	TEXTURE	FLAVOR
WHOLE GRAINS barley, farro, oats, quinoa (faux grain), rice, spelt, and more	*Grains are great for texture! From bouncy rice to crunchy oats, be careful not to blend the grains to a purée.*	*Grains have subtle flavors and are more useful for bulk and filling substance than flavoring. Toasting enhances grains with a nutty flavor.*
NUTS & SEEDS chia seeds, flaxseed, sesame seeds, almonds, cashews, macadamia nuts, pistachios, and walnuts	*Ground and crushed nuts give a crunchy texture to patties. Sprouted seeds add excellent texture!*	*Seeds and nuts add distinct flavor, which is enhanced by toasting before combine in the mixture.*
ROOT VEGETABLES beets, cabbages, carrots, cauliflower, fennel, potato, sweet potato, and turnips	*Roughly grated root vegetables add interesting texture.*	*Roots mostly have subtle flavors ranging from sweet to earthy. Carrots, sweet potatoes, and parsnips add sweetness while cauliflower and fennel are more pungent flavors.*
PULSES black beans, chickpeas, fava beans, lentils (black, green, and red), and white beans	*Be careful not to blend or mash pulses into a purée. Process for just a few seconds for a textured bite.*	*Beautiful but very subtle flavors that need to be supported by umami ingredients to shine!*
VEGETABLES bell peppers, eggplant, leafy greens, squashes, tomatoes, and zucchini	*Generally soft and need support from sturdier ingredients such as root vegetables and pulses.*	*Plenty of rich flavors can be found in peppers and tomatoes. Squashes are a little more subtle and need umami enhancement.*
UMAMI-RICH PLANTS garlic, mushrooms, onions, and seaweed	*Smooth and silky textures that need support from grains or/and pulses.*	*Your main sources for flavor! Umami carries the flavor for the whole patty!*
ADDING INTEREST capers, chile peppers, chili sauces, dairy cheeses, ghee, herbs, nutritional yeast, olives, soy sauce or tamari (umami), spice sauces, and sun-dried tomatoes	*Sauces, oils, peppers, dried herbs, and spices don't add much texture. However, sun-dried tomatoes, olives, and capers can add salty pieces that elevate a patty to heavenly heights!*	*Use these ingredients to create savory, sourness, and to add character to patties.*

FIRMNESS	JUICINESS	ADDITIONAL NOTES
The starch and texture of slightly broken-up grains are a natural glue for veggie burgers! Rescue a soggy mixture by adding more grains.	Grains absorb moisture and need to be balanced by juicy vegetables and liquids.	**Use whole grains for an extra health boost and a more powerful texture! Experiment with a variety of grains to discover their unique qualities.**
Chia seeds and flaxseed work well as egg substitutes: 1 tablespoon chia seeds (11 g) soaked in 3 tablespoons (45 ml) water for 15 minutes approximates 1 egg.	Nuts and seeds don't add juiciness when whole or in pieces, but ground nuts and seeds make creamy, oily pastes that can add extra savory juiciness to patties.	**Sprouted seeds are extra nutritious and add plenty of crunch!**
These generally don't help the burger hold together, but starchy potatoes and stringy grated root vegetables help bind when combined with pulses.	Root vegetables such as potatoes, especially sweet potatoes, beets, and carrots, add juiciness to patty mixes.	**Cauliflower has a stand-out flavor among root vegetables and can be roughly grated, finely diced, roasted, or panfried for maximum flavor.**
Beans, especially black beans, are great binders. Process them, being careful not to purée them. Lentils and chickpeas also bind, but less so than beans.	Cooked pulses add medium juiciness to patty mixes.	**Rinse and drain pulses well. Dry them on a towel or quickly heat them in a pan to reduce excess moisture.**
Not excellent for firmness, but vegetables work well together with grains and beans.	Lots of moistness and juiciness! Use sun-dried tomatoes instead of raw. These vegetables need to be heated to sweat out their water content before adding to a patty mixture.	**Fresh tomatoes are very moist and difficult to use in patties. Zucchini and eggplant need to be drained of excess moisture or they could make the mixture soggy.**
No great binding properties here.	Onions and mushrooms provide plenty of savory juices to patties. Sauté them to reduce moisture before adding to mixtures.	**Seaweed gives a seafood flavor to patties. Herbs are excellent for defining flavor.**
No great binding properties here either.	Sauce ingredients add delicious juiciness, as do oils, cheeses, olives, and sun-dried tomatoes.	**Taste the mixture and adjust with umami-enriching ingredients before shaping your patties.**

Acknowledgments

My friends and family. Thank you Natal, Nova, Evan, Jan, Leoni, Christo, and Fleur for contributing to this book in various ways. I couldn't have finished it without your enthusiasm and assistance. Also, many thanks to the wonderful team at Quarry Books, especially Jonathan, Anne, and Meredith. And, finally, a huge thank you to my friends in the blog and Instagram community from which I constantly draw inspiration: @tastyasheck, @ritaserano, @adelasterfoodtextures, @bettinaskitchen, @talinegabriel, @thesunshineeatery, @thelittleplantation, @rebelrecipes, @shisodelicious, @wholygoodness

About the Author

Nina Olsson founded NourishAtelier.com to share her passion for vegetarian cooking. For more than ten years, she has worked creatively with food as an award-winning art director, stylist, and designer. Her recipes have appeared in publications such as *Elle*, *Delicious*, and *Women's Health*. A native of Stockholm, Sweden, today Olsson lives along the coast of the North Sea in the Netherlands with her love Natal and their two children.

Index